"Helping people come close to God is a task for all Christians but notably spiritual directors and evangelists. *Learning the Language of the Soul* is imaginative equipment for this task drawing on Andrew Mayes's breadth and depth. There is novelty in this book restating past wisdom and engaging with the connected generation."

> — Canon John Twisleton is parish priest and theologian, author and Premier Radio presenter

"These pages offer wisdom, delight and an invitation—a creative exploration, a beckoning journey to bring alive our many encounters with God through symbol and imagery. *Learning the Language of the Soul* offers words for the sometimes silent mystery we name as God—a soulful, rich resource for spiritual directors and all seekers."

> — Sue Cash, Affiliated Sister of the Visitation, Spiritual Director, and Stillness and Silence Mentor

Learning the Language of the Soul

A Spiritual Lexicon

Andrew D. Mayes

LITURGICAL PRESS
Collegeville, Minnesota

www.litpress.org

Cover design by Monica Bokinskie. Cover image © Thinkstock.

1   2   3   4   5   6   7   8   9

Library of Congress Cataloging-in-Publication Data

Names: Mayes, Andrew D.
Title: Learning the language of the soul : a spiritual lexicon / Andrew D. Mayes.
Description: Collegeville, Minnesota : Liturgical Press, 2016. | Includes bibliographical references.
Identifiers: LCCN 2015028357| ISBN 9780814647523 | ISBN 9780814647516 (ebook)
Subjects: LCSH: Language and languages—Religious aspects—Christianity. | Metaphor—Religious aspects—Christianity. | Rhetoric—Religious aspects—Christianity. | Communication—Religious aspects—Christianity. | Metaphor in the Bible.
Classification: LCC BR115 .L25 M39 2016 | DDC 248.01/4—dc23
LC record available at https://lccn.loc.gov/2015028357

Contents

Preface

O world invisible, we view thee,
O world intangible, we touch thee.

—Francis Thompson,
"In No Strange Land"[1]

How can we describe to others what is happening to us on our spiritual journey? How can we depict, for the benefit of ourselves and for others, the spiritual road that we are taking: experiences of prayer, transitions that we travel through, and impediments that we face? How can we find images for the intangible, "naming" the invisible, bring to visualization the unseen, and express the silences? How can we externalize into words the interior emotions and movements in the soul? How can we learn spiritual fluency?

We find ourselves lost for words, tongue-tied, dumbfounded, and longing to find an expression. As the Jesuit spiritual directors William Barry and and William Connelly put it: "most people are inarticulate when they try . . . to describe their deeper feelings and attitudes. They can be even less articulate when they try to describe their relationship with God. . . . For to begin to talk about this aspect of their lives requires the equivalent of a new language, the ability to articulate inner experience."[2]

In the sixteenth century, the Spanish Franciscan Francisco de Osuna wrote: "some matters of mystical theology cannot be understood in ordinary language."[3] De Osuna composed three "spiritual alphabets" that introduced the seeker to key ways of approaching the passion, spiritual disciplines, and the practice of prayer. As his translator explains: "We must become as little children, learning our ABCs of spirituality."[4]

We need to equip and inspire *spiritual literacy*. We need to be able to read our soul. We need to access appropriate vocabulary for spiritual direction: images and pictures, often stunning and unnerving, that help us describe and clarify what is happening to us; language and terms that will develop our awareness, make the abstract concrete, and make transparent what is opaque and cloudy. We need interpretive frameworks. We need to develop proficiency in the use of appropriate language, linguistic competency.

The Aim of This Book

This book aims to be a sort of primer for the spiritual journey. The dictionary tells us that a *primer* has two major meanings: it can be a resource to help people to read (the word has been used for a basic prayer book) or it can be a person or material that primes, starting off a process—including an explosive charge that will ignite. Within this second range of meanings, a primer can prepare people for a situation so that they know what to do or say. This book aims to be a primer in all senses: to be a useful introduction to the art of reading the spiritual transitions that take place in people and finding words to express these; and a resource to inspire you and equip you in your spiritual journey, helping to ignite and spark off fruitful conversations about the inner changes. It is a kind of "vocab book" for students of spirituality, providing a wide range of terms and words that will be useful in conversations about the spiritual life, whether by spiritual directors—people who accompany others on their spiritual travel—or by any Christian who wants to reflect on his or her inner life and find words to describe it. So this book may serve as a kind of handbook for spiritual directors or soul friends. It may prove to be a great resource for evangelists and spiritual seekers, as well. With its questions for reflection, it will also be useful for groups—parish groups, for example, or supervision groups for spiritual directors. As the poet Micheal O'Siadhail puts it: "It seems that we have an innate facility to acquire language. There is good linguistic, and even genetic evidence, that we're hardwired to work language. Yet we never finish and never completely know even our own language. We go on learning all our lives. . . . We're endless language learners."[5]

Looking in Two Directions

We need to look in two directions: to the past and to the present. Many spiritual directors have little sense of their roots, the wider Christian history, and need to connect with the tradition, learning from spiritual writers from the past. Sheldrake reminds us that two horizons intersect: "What is needed is a receptive and at the same time critical dialogue with a spiritual text in order to allow the wisdom contained in it to challenge us and yet to accord our own horizons their proper place."[6] In this resource, we will alert the reader to the rich treasures of Christian spirituality over twenty centuries, helping us to reconnect with the tradition and appreciate and celebrate our roots and springs. We will discover images from every part of the Christian tradition: Catholic, Orthodox, Anglican/Episcopal, and Evangelical.

Where can we encounter the raw material of a divine–human relationship described by others? In what places might we find accounts of people's experience of prayer? How can we encounter the experiences of others? There is a wide range of genres, both traditional and contemporary, that we shall refer to in this book. Historic and classic sources include treatises, sermons, devotional manuals, pastoral and spiritual direction handbooks, discourses of spiritual direction, spiritual autobiography and personal history, and journals or reflection on experience. We shall look at monastic rules, stories and narratives, letters of spiritual direction, poems, ritual/ liturgical texts, and even art and music.

But we need also to relate to the culture of our time and place, connecting with contemporary images that speak powerfully in our own context. As renowned spiritual guide Carolyn Gratton put it: "A spiritual guide needs to be a skilled translator. People need to have guidance in the language of their own actual life state, whether they are academics or steelworkers, teenagers or senior citizens."[7]

We need to be like the householder of the kingdom, bringing out of our storeroom treasures both old and new (Matt 13:52). But Joseph Campbell cautions: "We must remember, however, that the metaphors of one historically conditioned period, and the symbols they innervate, may not speak to the persons who are living long after that historical moment and whose consciousness has been formed through altogether different experiences."[8] In this book, we shall discover contemporary sources that connect us with the experience of young people, and we shall discover arresting images in song books, worship texts, and guides to spiritual life, finding metaphors that emerge in today's movies and technology.

Biblical scholar Sandra Schneiders, too, reminds us of the importance of context in shaping religious language appropriate to the time and place.[9] Nevertheless, we shall see that the metaphors we encounter here turn out to be archetypal and resonate with our souls across the centuries and cultures. Theologian John Hick reminds us: "the effectiveness of metaphor as a form of communication depends upon a common reservoir of shared associations,"[10] and it is the purpose of this book to lead the reader to the reservoir or pool of images that inspire spiritual communication.

This book aims to be a kind of modern dictionary of the soul, paying tribute to classical images that are a cherished part of our tradition and exploring some contemporary idioms of the spiritual life. People need help to find the appropriate language in prayer; we need a book on *Holy Speaking* to complement Margaret Guenther's *Holy Listening*.[11] After an opening introductory chapter exploring the significance of metaphors, we shall explore these types of images:

- familial, relational language of sons and daughters, sensual language of friends and lovers, metaphors of tenderness and risk, metaphors of baptismal identity, and a look at the question of inclusive language for the deity;
- horticultural, agricultural, and temporal metaphors;
- musical and dynamic metaphors;
- geographical and topographical metaphors;
- architectural and spatial metaphors;
- metaphors of physicality and spirituality;
- elemental, raw, meteorological metaphors;
- metaphors of the spiritual combat;
- edgy metaphors arising from our contemporary culture;

and we conclude with the invitation to cease talking, moving beyond images into wordless silence!

Using This Book

For whom is this book written? This resource equips spiritual directors and all who desire to expand their spiritual vocabulary. It is a useful tool for spiritual directors' supervision groups and their ongoing training. It is for evangelists and all involved in witnessing to our faith in today's world. It is not for putting words into your mouth but rather for opening new vistas, new perspectives, and fresh ways of seeing things. It is an invitation to deeper prayer, for as Kathleen Fischer observes:

> Integrating a new image into prayer is a different process from ana-
> lyzing its adequacy from a theological perspective. . . . The process
> of integrating new images into our spiritual lives involves not only
> talking about new metaphors, but praying to God under these new
> names, seeing self and world through these images . . . a symbol or

image achieves power in the spiritual life by gradually unfolding its significance.[12]

This resource will help you rediscover a range of metaphors to enable you to

- activate and stimulate prayer, facilitate discernment, and clarify perceptions;
- animate and gently explore feelings and responses experienced in prayer;
- communicate an aspect of the divine and articulate your longings;
- illustrate with a well-chosen image, and cast fresh light on the discovery of God;
- formulate the intangible experience of God into words;
- investigate further words that a directee has used and ask probing questions;
- navigate the waters of the soul and its journey;
- liberate your spirit and germinate your ideas;
- experiment with playfulness and stimulate creativity

Acknowledgements

Unless otherwise noted, scripture texts in this work are taken from the *New Revised Standard Version Bible* © 1989, 1993, Division of Christian Education of the National Council of the Churches of Christ in the United States of America. Used by permission. All rights reserved.

Scripture quotations marked (*Jerusalem Bible*) from *The Jerusalem Bible* © 1966 by Darton Longman & Todd Ltd and Doubleday and Company Ltd.

Scripture quotations marked (*The Voice*) taken from The Voice™. Copyright © 2008 by Ecclesia Bible Society. Used by permission. All rights reserved.

Scripture quotations marked (CEV) are from the Contemporary English Version Copyright © 1991, 1992, 1995 by American Bible Society, Used by Permission.

Scripture quotations marked (CEB) are taken from the Common English Bible, copyright 2011. Used by permission. All rights reserved.

Scripture quotations marked (*The Message*) copyright © by Eugene H. Peterson 1993, 1994, 1995, 1996, 2000, 2001, 2002. Used by permission of NavPress. All rights reserved. Represented by Tyndale House Publishers, Inc.

Scripture quotations marked (NCV) taken from the New Century Version®. Copyright © 2005 by Thomas Nelson. Used by permission. All rights reserved.

Scripture quotations marked (NIV) are taken from the Holy Bible, New International Version®, NIV®. Copyright © 1973, 1978, 1984, 2011 by Biblica, Inc.™ Used by permission of Zondervan. All rights reserved worldwide. www.zondervan.com The "NIV" and "New International Version" are trademarks registered in the United States Patent and Trademark Office by Biblica, Inc.™

Excerpt from "Praise Like Fireworks" and "Christ Has Set Me Free" by Rend Collective Experiment © Thankyou Music. Used with permission.

Excerpt from "God of Concrete, God of Steel" by Richard G. Jones © 1968 Stainer & Bell, Ltd. (Admin. Hope Publishing Company, Carol Stream, IL 60188). All rights reserved. Used by permission.

Excerpt from "Tongues" from Micheal O'Siadhail, *Collected Poems*. Bloodaxe Books, 2013. Reproduced with permission of Bloodaxe Books on behalf of the author. www.bloodaxebooks.com.

The poem "Fulness of Life" from Stephen Cherry, *Barefoot Prayers* (London: SPCK, 2013).

Excerpt from *Meditations with Meister Eckhart*. Edted by Matthew Fox. Inner Traditions and Bear & Company © 2001. All rights reserved. www .Innertraditions.com. Reprinted with permission of publisher.

Excerpt from *The Luminous Eye: The Spiritual World Vision of St. Ephrem the Syrian*, Sebastian Brock. Cistercian Publications, Kalamazoo, Michigan, 1992 and Liturgical Press, Collegeville, Minnesota. Reprinted with permission.

1

Mystic Metaphors

> Here we sense the function of
> metaphor that allows us to make
> a journey we could not otherwise
> make.
>
> — Joseph Campbell [1]

As we seek to bring to expression aspects of our inner, spiritual life, we discover that we need metaphors, frameworks, and reference points. Theologian Jürgen Moltmann affirms how vital it is to use metaphors or images to describe the spiritual experience: "In the mystical metaphors, the distance between a transcendent subject and its immanent work is ended . . . the divine and human are joined in an organic cohesion." [2]

Appreciating Metaphor: Extreme Language?

Sue Pickering writes in her useful resource *Spiritual Direction: A Practical Introduction*: "By noticing metaphorical language we can help directees connect not only with their thinking but also with their emotional life and we can wonder together where God might be in the midst of their circumstances . . . helping our directees use their imagination to unpack levels of meaning contained in a symbol is exciting work." [3]

As we access feelings and aspects of our godward relationship by metaphor, we stumble on insights that we cannot approach in a more analytical or abstract conceptual mode. They open up rich canyons to explore both by directee and director. Janet Ruffing notices the natural emergence of metaphor in the sharing of stories and experiences between directee and director:

> By uncovering the latent meanings and logical implications of the
> images and symbols emerging in the spiritual-direction conversation,

1

we glimpse the plot and affective attitudes implicit in this language. We often say more than we fully grasp when such feeling words and images pour out of our mouths. Examining the dominant symbols and patterns of imagery with people in direction gives them access to what they already know about themselves in some vague way. . . . Sensitive direction requires the director to invite sufficient elaboration of the significant key images or symbols to ensure the possibility of grasping their meanings.[4]

The use of metaphors in expressing Christian insights is inescapable. Theologian Paul Avis argues: "All the significant assertions of theology are expressed in a language that is irreducibly metaphorical."[5] Avis points out that metaphors drawn from the natural world are used by poets as a hermeneutical key to help map the landscapes of the mind: "Metaphor is generated in the drive to understand experience. . . . Metaphor is not just naming one thing in terms of another, but seeing, experiencing and intellectualizing one thing in the light of the other."[6] There is also a heuristic potential in metaphors; they help us discover new ideas in the exploration of an issue. As hymnist Brian Wren puts it: "Metaphors can organize language, encourage a transfer of associations and feelings between the matrices they intersect, extend language, generate new insights, and move us at a deep level by their appeal to the senses and imagination."[7] Metaphors have the power to shift us from left-brain analytical thinking to creative right-hemisphere imagining—and imaging.

Theologian Sallie McFague claims a creative role for metaphor in theology. She points out that metaphor is not just a useful literary device bringing color into description; it can actually enable knowledge and understanding that could not be gained by other ways. In *Metaphorical Theology* she argues that models allow insights prompted by metaphor to be related in practical ways to Christian discipleship.[8] From a different perspective Walter Brueggemann points to the creative use of imagery in the Old Testament prophets, making possible the emergence of an alternative perception of reality. Inspired imagination, often using metaphor, enables things to be seen differently and even opens up new futures.[9] The use of metaphor to describe prayer respects the mystery and elusive character of prayer.

In his recent study *The Edge of Words: God and the Habits of Language*, Rowan Williams affirms: "So as we take more risks and propose more innovations in our linguistic practice, we move from the more-or-less illustrative use of a vivid and unusual simile through to increasingly explosive usages that ultimately . . . invite us to rethink our metaphysical principles, our sense of how intelligible identities are constructed in and for our speaking. Extreme or apparently excessive speech is not an aberration in our speaking." [10] Richard Harries writes of this study: "We may find ourselves looking for a new kind of language altogether, one in a different register which shifts our whole understanding . . . a different mode . . . we might come to utter some stammering words about God." [11]

How Metaphors Work

The limit of metaphor and its provisionality must be recognized alongside its potential for communicating insights. Gunton argues that metaphor in theology can indeed express the significance of what is happening (in atonement, for example) and open up a conversation: "We encounter not *mere* metaphors but linguistic usages which demand a new way of thinking about and living in the world." [12] From a literary perspective, William Countryman notes how metaphor and lyric poetry play a part in exploring experiences associated with prayer, offering "a point of comparison and perhaps illumination . . . an opportunity to discourse about the hidden, interior realities of spirituality." [13] Metaphors trigger the imagination. Theologian John Macquarrie reminds us that symbols and concepts need each other: "We speak of the Holy Spirit not only in the symbols mentioned above [wind, fire, water] but also in such concepts as creativity, procession, unification . . . we find theological language displaying a dialectical character, employing both images and concepts, and allowing them to interpret each other." [14]

The communication of ideas in a postmodern world favors the image over the metanarrative. [15] Metaphors have "added value," not only illustrating but illuminating; they aid in description but also stimulate insights. In *The Analogical Imagination* theologian David Tracy affirms that in experiencing an encounter with Christ, the Christian must move through the range of Christian forms and symbols in order to find suitable expression for the significance of this event. [16] Reflection on experience, Tracy says, can be expressed in one of two ways: either using analogical language and metaphor or using dialectical language that emphasizes the theme of negation in Christian theology.

Theologian Janet Martin Soskice reminds us of the three types of theory regarding how metaphors function. *Substitution* theories suggest that a metaphor takes the place of a literal term and becomes something of a perplexing riddle. *Emotive* theories affirm that a metaphor resonates strongly with our feelings and evokes and expresses the affective or emotional side of our experience. But it is the *incremental* theories that are most inspirational. They affirm that metaphors have a cognitive role, aiding and deepening our understanding of things: "What is said by the metaphor can be expressed adequately in no other way . . . the combination of parts in a metaphor can produce new and unique agents of meaning." [17] Metaphors evoke and stimulate rather than define or confine. Metaphors help to unify and integrate experience, because they link the spiritual to the physical and the soul to the body, enabling the metaphysical to become physical.

Seeing Things Differently: Prayer and Perception

George Herbert calls prayer "the soul in paraphrase," and Rowan Williams describes contemplative prayer as involving "the project of reconditioning perception." [18] Psychologists Fraser Watts and Mark Williams, in their study *The Psychology of Religious Knowing*, are cautious about assigning a directly cognitive role to prayer, but they acknowledge that in prayer we need to organize and reorganize our thoughts and priorities: "Indeed it is doubtful whether the 'acquisition of knowledge' is at all an appropriate way to describe the cognitive changes that take place in prayer. Prayer is probably better described as the *reinterpretation* of what is in some sense already known than as an exercise in the acquisition of knowledge." [19]

For Williams and Watts, prayer is "an exercise in the interpretation of experience." [20] As another psychologist of religion puts it: "to decipher inner thoughts is therefore part of the practice of prayer." [21] This resonates with prayer as discernment, a theme that will surface throughout this book. Ann and Barry Ulanov describe prayer as "primary speech" in the sense that in prayer a person can talk freely with unguarded honesty of his or her deepest desires, fears, fantasies, misconceptions, and confusions: "This is what depth-psychologists call 'primary-process thinking,' that level of our psyche's functioning that leads straight to the workings of our souls." [22] For them prayer is the naked exposure of the soul to God, which entails an experience of transformation they describe in terms of transfiguration: "This means we are living now in rearranged form. We are the same persons and yet radically different. . . . The theme that dominates our lives now is the effort to correspond with grace. We want to go with the little signs and fragments of new being given us in prayer." [23]

Prayer entails the risk of change, in which, little by little, perceptions are revised, self-acceptance grows, and contradictions, if not resolved, become better understood.

Vocalizing our Experiences

Pastoral theologian Tjeu van Knippenberg reminds us that there is a transition between the actual "raw experience" and the way it comes to light through the later sharing of a narrative with the spiritual director or soul friend.[24] He draws attention to four stages in interpretation (or hermeneutic levels) that play a role in the description of prayer or configuration of a personal narrative on prayer. First, we have unarticulated experiences and events that have not yet been explicitly formulated in terms of time and space. Second, we relate to ourselves a "story-in-itself" about our personal experiences, like an internal private diary that makes sense only to us. Next begins a process of "recalibrating" or "reconfiguring" the story in interaction with the narratives of others and drawing on available images and metaphors. Fourth, this enables one to assess one's experience against the background of the tradition or collective narrative and begin to make sense of it. This is a helpful reminder that the prayer experience passes, as it were, through different levels of consciousness and interpretation before it can be described to another person.[25] Joseph Campbell, in similar vein, has pointed out that the most important thing about any spiritual or peak experience is the raw experience itself. The second crucial thing is what we tell ourselves the experience means and how we fit it into our beliefs and past experiences. The third challenge is the process of explaining our experience to others.[26]

Philosopher Caroline Franks Davis reminds us that all experience is interpreted within "a continual interplay between concepts, beliefs, events, reflection, the creative imagination, and other cognitive and perceptual factors."[27] All subjects make sense of their experience, for themselves and in communicating their experience to others, through "perceptual sets" influenced by language, culture, and context; we draw on a bank or reservoir of images.[28] The spiritual director or listener needs to be alert to the thought-world of the directee and appreciate that the directee's interpretations actually add understanding to her or his experience.

Rediscovering the Power of Words

We also need to rediscover the sacramentality of words: like bread and wine they can bear God's presence and reveal the divine, so words should be approached with reverence and appreciation. It has been said that we live in a *googlesque* world: we are bombarded by facts, data, and cheap words, but what is needed is not information but *inner formation*, where our language arises from a deep place, the place of encounter with God. In the practice of prayer, language inspires—not necessarily instructing or informing—and we notice how Jesus in his parables emerges as a poet, teaching not by defining but by evoking our imaginations. The Bible is brimming with images of salvation: the concepts of reconciliation, redemption, and sacrifice all depend on the power of metaphor. Soskice affirms: "The sacred literature . . . both records the experiences of the past and provides the descriptive language by which any new experience may be interpreted."[29] The Bible is the primary source of our mystic metaphors, standing at the fountainhead of the river of images that courses through history.

In recent years there has been a return to metaphor in the language of our worship and liturgy. The Church of England has left behind the functionalist and prosaic language of the *Alternative Services Book* (1980) and moved to the poetic and evocative language of *Common Worship* (2000). Where once we endured phrases like: "It is our duty and our joy . . . to give you thanks and praise" (*Alternative Services Book* , Eucharistic Prayer 2), now we encounter language that lifts and stirs our spirits: "all your works echo the silent music of your praise" (*Common Worship*, Eucharistic Prayer G). Funeral prayers now connect more tenderly with the feelings of the bereaved:

> God our Father,
> in loving care your hand has created us,
> and as the potter fashions the clay
> you have formed us in your image . . .
> hold before us our beginning and our ending,
> the dust from which we come
> and the death to which we move, . . .[30]

One contemporary prayer in the Anglican (English) funeral rite acknowledges:

> We scarcely know the words to speak . . .
> When all is pain, we long for help.

In the Daily Office the bland invitation of the *Alternative Services Book*, "Let us worship the Lord: All praise to his name," is replaced in *Common Worship* by

> Blessed are you, Lord our God, redeemer and king of all . . .
> From the waters of chaos you drew forth your world . . .

In this sense, there has been a return to the poetic thought-world of the *Book of Common Prayer* (1662), famous for its evocative phrasing and cadences written by Thomas Cranmer (1489–1556), as in the prayer marking the beginning of the Christian year, the first Sunday of Advent:

> Almighty God, give us grace that we may cast away the works of darkness, and put upon us the armor of light, now in the time of this mortal life, in which thy Son Jesus Christ came to visit us in great humility; that in the last day, when he shall come again in his glorious Majesty, to judge both the quick and the dead, we may rise to the life immortal; through him who liveth and reigneth with thee and the Holy Ghost, now and ever. Amen.

There has been a similar shift in the Roman Catholic Church as the Latin Mass has been newly translated in favor of richer language: the banal "And also with you" response has been replaced in 2011 with "And with your spirit." The response to the invitation to communion has been freshly translated in order to evoke traditional imagery: "Lord, I am not worthy that you should enter under my roof, but only say the word and my soul shall be healed." The Rite for the Blessing and Sprinkling of Water now poetically reads: "Renew the living spring of your grace within us and grant that by this water we may be defended from all ills of spirit and body, and so approach you with hearts made clean and worthily receive your salvation." [31]

In the fourth century Mesrop Mashtots invented the Armenian alphabet in order to communicate to his people the Christian message, and in the ninth century the saints Cyril and Methodius designed an alphabet (later called the Cyrillic) to bring the Orthodox faith to the Slavic people. In every generation we need alphabets and metaphors that connect with our experience. As we shall see, archetypal images endure powerfully, but as the spiritual writer Jean Maalouf has recently said, "Every few years, we have to retranslate the Bible. Every few years, we have to retranslate a book, even and maybe especially the Bible. Every few years, we have to rewrite a dictionary. The same words don't convey the same message in succeeding situations and for different generations." [32]

Questions for Reflection and Discussion

1. What images come to mind when you start to think about God?

2. What metaphors arise in your consciousness when you begin to describe the course of your spiritual life over the last year?

3. What kind of metaphors do you tend to use most easily? (You might consider the list in the Preface). Why is that?

4. Sue Pickering writes: "We can wonder together where God might be." What can stimulate the art of wondering—reflection and musing—about God's presence in your life?

Further Reading

Fischer, Kathleen. *The Inner Rainbow: The Imagination in Christian Life.* Mahwah, NJ: Paulist, 1983.

Nilsen, Mary Ylvisaker. *Words That Sing: Composing Lyrical Prose.* Des Moines, IA: Zion, 2012.

Williams, Rowan. *The Edge of Words: God and the Habits of Language.* London: Bloomsbury, 2014.

Wren, Brian. *What Language Shall I Borrow? God-Talk in Worship.* London: SCM, 1989.

2

The Tender and Risky Language of Children, Friends, Lovers

"What language shall I borrow to thank Thee, dearest friend!"

— O Sacred Head Once Wounded,
attributed to Bernard of Clairvaux

In this chapter we explore social and personal metaphors that emerge from our human relationships, and we begin to consider how appropriate they are for describing or representing the divine–human encounter. Eugene Peterson reminds us of the need of such language:

> Informational language and motivational language dominate our society. We are well schooled in language that describes the world in which we live. We are well trained in language that moves people to buy and join and vote. Meanwhile . . . the language of intimacy languishes. Once we are clear of the cradle, we find less and less occasion to use it. . . . Prayer is [such] language.[1]

The Language of God's Children: Daughters and Sons

At the very foundation of our spiritual life lies the awesome truth of our baptismal identity: we are the sons and daughters of God. Jesus Christ our elder brother brings us into this filial relationship whereby we can call God our Father. Paul declares: "But when the fullness of time had come, God sent his Son, born of a woman, born under the law, in order to redeem those who were under the law, so that we might receive adoption as children. And because you are children, God has sent the Spirit of his Son into our hearts, crying, 'Abba! Father!' So you are no longer a slave but a child, and if a child then also an heir, through God" (Gal 4:4-7). He spells the relationship out: "For all who are led by the Spirit of God are children of God. For you did not receive a spirit of slavery to fall back into fear, but you have received a spirit of adoption. When we cry, 'Abba! Father!' it is that very Spirit bearing witness with our spirit that we are children of God" (Rom 8:14-16).

This is the primary and most basic metaphor: God is our Father and we his children. We claim for ourselves the affirmation that Jesus experienced at his baptism in the Father's voice: 'You are my beloved Son; with you I am well pleased!'

The first building block of our relationship with God: to develop a relationship with the heavenly Father. As Jesus becomes our brother, we discover our dignity and vocation. Jesus greets his disciples as his own brothers and sisters: "pointing to his disciples, he said, 'Here are my mother and my brothers! For whoever does the will of my Father in heaven is my brother and sister and mother'" (Matt 12:49-50; Mark 3:33). We discover Jesus as our brother when we do God's will. Paul and other writers suggest that Jesus is the *eldest* brother: "the firstborn within a large family" (Rom 8:29). As Colossians puts it: "He is the image of the invisible God, the firstborn of all creation" (Col 1:15), and the letter to the Hebrews assures us in these terms that Jesus is our brother:

> the one who sanctifies and those who are sanctified all have one Father. For this reason Jesus is not ashamed to call them brothers and sisters, saying, "I will proclaim your name to my brothers and sisters, in the midst of the congregation I will praise you." Since, therefore, the children share flesh and blood, he himself likewise shared the same things . . . he had to become like his brothers and sisters in every respect, so that he might be a merciful and faithful high priest in the service of God. (Heb 2:11–3:1)

Jesus calls us to rediscover spiritual childhood: "I tell you, whoever does not receive the kingdom of God as a little child will never enter it" (Mark 10:15). He is emphatic: "Truly I tell you, unless you change and become like children, you will never enter the kingdom of heaven" (Matt 18:3). This is a call to spiritual playfulness, to spontaneity, and we recall that in the first-century mindset of honor and shame children were social nobodies cherished and valued by Christ.[2] But thinking of ourselves as spiritual children is not all carefree fun. We can be unruly, and we wonder to ourselves how to make sense of difficult things happening to us. The letter to the Hebrews offers one explanation in terms of the Father training us:

And you have forgotten the exhortation that addresses you as children—
"My child, do not regard lightly the discipline of the Lord,
   or lose heart when you are punished by him;
for the Lord disciplines those whom he loves
   and chastises every child whom he accepts."

Endure trials for the sake of discipline. God is treating you as children; for what child is there whom a parent does not discipline? If you do not have that discipline in which all children share, then you are illegitimate and not his children. Moreover, we had human parents to discipline us, and we respected them. Should we not be even more willing to be subject to the Father of spirits and live? For they disciplined us for a short time as seemed best to them, but he disciplines us for our good, in order that we may share his holiness. Now, discipline always seems painful rather than pleasant at the time, but later it yields the peaceful fruit of righteousness to those who have been trained by it. (Heb 12:5-10)

If God is to be imaged as Father, male language needs to be complemented by feminine imagery. Paul puts it:

For in Christ Jesus you are all children of God through faith. As many of you as were baptized into Christ have clothed yourselves with Christ. There is no longer Jew or Greek, there is no longer slave or free, there is no longer male and female; for all of you are one in Christ Jesus. (Gal 3.26-28)

Paul himself leads the way! In his earliest epistle, Paul places two images of spiritual support side by side:

We were gentle among you, like a nurse tenderly caring for her children. . . . As you know, we dealt with each one of you like a father with his children urging and encouraging you and pleading that you lead a life worthy of God, who calls you into his own kingdom and glory. (1 Thess 2:7, 11-12)

In the Old Testament, there are intimations that another way of looking at the relationship may be possible. While there is a propensity for male patriarchal language—God is considered to be "a rock, a fortress, my strong tower, my shield" (Ps 144:2)—sometimes more tender language breaks through:

But I have calmed and quieted my soul,
like a weaned child with its mother;
my soul is like the weaned child that is with me. (Ps 131:2)

Three times the prophet Isaiah places into God's mouth such striking feminine imagery:

> For a long time I have held my peace,
>   I have kept still and restrained myself;
> now I will cry out like a woman in labor,
>   I will gasp and pant.
> Can a woman forget her nursing-child,
>   or show no compassion for the child of her womb?
> Even these may forget, yet I will not forget you . . .
> As a mother comforts her child,
>   so I will comfort you. (Isa 42:14; 49:15; 66:13)

While he delights in God his "Abba Father" (Mark 14:36) and in the parable of the Prodigal images God as a father on tiptoe for the return of his wayward child, Jesus himself uses feminine imagery at least six times. He expresses his longing for the people of Jerusalem: "How often have I desired to gather your children together as a hen gathers her brood under her wings, and you were not willing!" (Luke 13:34).

Jesus uses feminine language in explicating his central theme, the reign of God. He says God's reign is like a woman hiding yeast within the dough (Matt 13:33). The reign of God is like the joy that a woman experiences when she finds something like a precious coin that got lost (Luke 15:8). In John's gospel (3:3), Jesus affirms that it is not possible to see God's kingdom unless one undergoes a new birth—a reference to divine mothering, perhaps? Daringly, Jesus likens the hour of his passion to childbirth (John 16:21-22), and of wars and rumors of wars he says: "But all these things are merely the beginning of birth pangs" (Matt 24:4-8), an image Paul takes up in Romans 8.

Julian of Norwich (1342–1416) encourages us to rediscover a mothering God who longs and yearns for us, overflowing with grace. It comes to her as a great revelation:

> Our good Lord showed me a spiritual sight of his familiar love. I saw
> that he is to us everything which is good and comforting for our help.
> He is our clothing, who wraps and enfolds us for love, embraces us
> and shelters us, surrounds us for his love, which is so tender that he
> may never desert us.[3]

In order to communicate this tenderness and compassion of God, Julian boldly employs the image of Christ as "mother." Drawing an analogy with human parenting, she teaches that Christ cherishes us as his own beloved children, longing to protect us, nurture us, and delight in us. Julian urges us to leave behind harsh images of God—like God the stern schoolmaster or God the wrathful judge:

> This fair lovely word "mother" is so sweet and so kind in itself that it cannot truly be said of anyone or to anyone except of him and to him who is the true Mother of life and of all things. . . . And when we fall, quickly he raises us up with his loving embrace and his gracious touch. And when we are strengthened by his sweet working, then we willingly choose him by his grace, that we shall be his servants and his lovers, constantly and forever.[4]

Julian suggests we need to unlearn some of our concepts of self and of God. We need to ponder God and humanity in the light of God's generosity and grace. If God is "courteous" toward us, we need to practice a similar respect and tolerance toward ourselves and others. We need to be gentle with ourselves and remember that God's grace respects our personality and individuality. We need to be ourselves, as God enables us to grow into the people the divine will calls us to be, deeply loved and animated by the Spirit.

Spiritual writer Henri Nouwen noticed, in his survey of prayers by young men at Yale University in the late 1960s, that there is often a movement from macho images of God to more sensitive ideas. He observed a transition from confusion to hope in a spectrum that moved from "the big buddy God" to "a compassionate God." Of the former Nouwen writes: "You can speak to God in a shoulder slapping way"; of the latter he notes: "These prayers can best be called anti-heroic prayers . . . they are prayers to a compassionate God, who does not ask for heroic martyrdom but wants to embrace a weak man."[5]

As Kathleen Fischer puts it:

> We are in the midst of an unprecedented revolution in our language for God. . . . Because of the reciprocal relationship between language and experience, religious experience is not only conditioned by, but also shapes, our language for the divine. A variety of approaches to expanding our language for God is then essential.[6]

Critique and Appreciation

The language of fatherhood in the divine can encourage both tenderness and a sense of authority. Of course the use of such images will be shaped and colored by own experience of a human father. For those who have suffered abuse or an authoritarian style of parenting the image can potentially become healing and restorative.

God is the father we never had, who enfolds us with unconditional compassion and respect. Spiritual writer Richard Rohr believes that the vast majority of people in the West suffer from what he calls "the father wound"—they have never been touched by a human father, maybe because he had died, was absent or aloof, or preoccupied with work. Rohr affirms that the reason God reveals himself as Father is because that is where most people are wounded or unwhole.[7]

The challenge in Christian spirituality is to balance ultimacy with intimacy, the divine as both transcendent and immanent: "Father in heaven" is complemented by "thy kingdom come" in the Lord's Prayer. Our liturgies persist in retaining not only male imagery but imagery that implies power and domination, and we notice how our images of God affect our images of self: "Lord" requires a servant, "King" requires an obedient subject, "Almighty" encourages us to be subservient and powerless. But feminine imagery is slowly coming into Anglican liturgy. Now *Common Worship* gives us this text in Eucharistic Prayer G:

> How wonderful the work of your hands, O Lord
> As a mother tenderly gathers her children,
> You embraced a people as your own.

Morning Prayer (Monday) offers us this dramatic prayer:

> When we turned away to darkness and chaos
> Like a mother you would not forsake us.
> You cried out like a woman in labor,
> And rejoiced to bring forth a new people.[8]

We need to be more alert as to the effect that certain images of God have on our own self-understanding. Language that excludes reciprocity may make it harder for us to cooperate with the grace of God except welcoming it in a passive way. The New Testament epistles occasionally delight in the language of synergy working together with God (Phil 2:13), and now we explore images that foster mutuality and human–divine partnership fostering communion, sharing and immediacy, rather than encouraging a sense of awe, distance, and overwhelming Otherness.

The Language of Friends and Lovers

God Our Friend

"I do not call you servant any longer, because the servant does not know what the master is doing; but I have called you friends, because I have made known to you everything that I have heard from my Father" (John 15:12-15). The beloved disciple lying on the breast of Jesus gives us a vivid image of this relationship. Jesus is hailed as "the friend of tax collectors" (Matt 11:19). Joseph Scriven's classic hymn celebrates this in devotional terms:

> What a friend we have in Jesus all my sins and griefs to bear. . . .
> Can we find a friend so faithful who will all our sorrows share?

The Passiontide hymn *My Song Is Love Unknown* puts it:

> Here might I stay and sing
> No story so divine. . . .
> This is my friend in whose sweet praise
> I all my days could gladly spend.

Friendship is marked by mutual attraction, reciprocity, mutuality, solidarity, and the honest sharing of emotions and concerns. It expresses itself in accepting a common mission, mutual commitment, and loyalty. In children, it is characterized by a delight to play together.

Aelred, Abbot of Rievaulx (1110–67) celebrated spiritual friendship as a clue to divine–human relationship in his work *De spiritali amicitia*, affirming that "God is friendship." Writing of friendship between humans, he suggests that here is a vocabulary that reveals the divine–human encounter: "Friendship is the twinning of minds and spirits where two become one. Your friend is a second self from whom you withhold nothing, hide nothing, fear nothing. . . . We ascend from that love, already holy, with which we embrace our friend, to the love with which we embrace Christ, this savouring joyfully and freely the fruit of spiritual friendship." [9] Aelred quotes St. Ambrose's words: "So if you have a friend, bare your whole heart to him and he will do the same for you, for a friend keeps nothing back. If he is a true friend he pours out his soul as the Lord Jesus poured out the secrets of the Father." [10]

God Our Lover

> You have seduced me, Yahweh,
> and I have let myself be seduced. (Jer 20:7, *Jerusalem Bible*)

> I am going to lure her
> And lead her out into the wilderness
> And speak to her heart. (Hos 2:16, *Jerusalem Bible*)

Already in the Old Testament, as the relationship between Israel and her God was clarified in terms of a marriage covenant, erotic and sensual language communicates an intensity of desire in the heart of both parties. Indeed, the language of intimacy pervades the Old Testament. Daringly, God is depicted as a lover:

> You shall no more be termed Forsaken,
>   and your land shall no more be termed Desolate;
> but you shall be called My Delight Is in Her,
>   and your land Married;
> for the LORD delights in you,
>   and your land shall be married.
> For as a young man marries a young woman,
>   so shall your builder marry you,
> and as the bridegroom rejoices over the bride,
>   so shall your God rejoice over you. (Isa 62:4-5)

This is taken to depths of a longing, passionate love in the sensuality of the *Song of Songs*. Though this collection of love poems does not mention God, the divine presence is energizing the relationship. The Song not only uses erotic language, but it also develops the theme of hide and seek, the presence and absence of the lover, and so the emotions of both communion and distress are explored. It moves from lines like "You have ravished my heart, my sister, my bride, you have ravished my heart with a glance of your eyes" (4:9) to "I sought him, but did not find him; I called him, but he gave no answer" (5:6).

Through the centuries spiritual writers have delighted in relational and social metaphors that enable them to explore the themes of spiritual dialogue and intimacy with God. A key theme is *eros* as desire for God. This is explored by Augustine, who experiences for himself in the *Confessions* that "our hearts will always be restless until they come to rest in God." As Marilyn Sewell observes: "The sacred is not in the sky, the place of transcendent, abstract principle, but rather is based on this earth, in the ordinary dwelling places of our lives, in our gardens and kitchens and bedrooms . . . and in our places of protest . . . the sacred is fuelled by eros, by desire. It is about passion. And compassion. And love. Always love." [11]

The Song of Songs became a rich inspiration for spiritual writers from Origen (third century) onwards; it was he who began the long tradition of reading this text as a description of the mystical relationship between Christ and the soul. Gregory of Nyssa (fourth century) approached the text through the lens of neoplatonism and so was unable to appreciate the sheer physicality of the poems but felt the need to spiritualize and allegorize them.[12]

Bernard of Clairvaux (1090–1153) traces a certain progression as he preaches on the topic "What it is to kiss the Lord's feet, hands and lips":

> This is the way and the order that must be followed. First, we fall at the feet of the Lord our Creator and lament our sins and faults. Second, we seek his helping hand to lift us up. . . . Third . . . we may perhaps dare to lift up our eyes and view the Lord's glorious and majestic face. We are not only to adore him, but we are (and I say this with fear and trembling) to kiss him . . . made to be one Spirit in him.[13]

Richard of St. Victor (d. 1173) describes a "steep stairway of love" with four stages in the relationship: betrothal, which corresponds with the stage of mystical purgation; courtship, signifying mystical illumination; wedlock, the unitive stage; and the fruitfulness of conjugal relations, where the mystic Bride becomes "a parent of fresh spiritual life." Richard "saw clearly that the union of the soul with its Source could not be a barren ecstasy."[14] The key in this narrative is the redirecting of erotic passion toward God, which includes sometimes very vivid sexual, pregnancy, and birthing imagery.

Meister Eckhart (thirteenth century) writes even more daringly than Richard, of giving birth to Christ from this naked immersion in Godhead—of the virgin becoming a wife and then of embodying and exuding the very compassion and justice of God, within which she is immersed in this most intimate union with God. He writes:

> From all eternity
>   God lies on a maternity bed
>   Giving birth.
> The essence of God is birthing.

And he asks:

> What good is it to me
> for the Creator to give birth to his/her son
> if I do not also give birth to him
> in my time
> and my culture?[15]

In the thirteenth century the Beguines pioneered the use of erotic and sensual language to describe one's relationship with divinity. The metaphors of lovemaking and intimacy not only embody the "grammar of desire" and positive emotions. Such images can also be vehicles for negative feelings within the evolving relationship: a sense of failure, of disappointment or frustration, of puzzling absence as well as passionate presence. Hadewijch, a Dutch Beguine, sings of unrequited love:

> He who lives on love with no success
> Endures, in the madness of love,
> Suffering that can only be known
> By him who sincerely forsakes all for Love,
> And then remains unnourished by her.
> He is in woe because of Love;
> For he sorely burns
> In hope and in fear
> Incessantly renewed.[16]

A contemporary at the same convent at Helfta, Saxony, Gertrude the Great, relates in her *Spiritual Exercises* a vision of Christ in which he says to her soul: "Why are you troubled my love? For as often as you desire it, I, the sovereign priest and true pontiff, will enter you. . . . I feed you with myself in the superfluity of my charity, and satisfy you with delights; and I penetrate your entire being like ointment by the sweetness of my spirit." [17]

In his *Spiritual Canticle* St. John of the Cross (b. 1542) takes this imagery to new depths of intensity and passion. He sees the human–divine relationship moving from spiritual betrothal to spiritual marriage, union, and consummation:

> In the inner wine cellar
> I drank of my Beloved. . .
> There he gave me his breast;
> There he taught me a sweet and living knowledge;
> I gave myself to him,
> Keeping nothing back;
> There I promised to be his bride.[18]

Interpreters today shy away from allegorical approaches to the text of the Song of Songs and rather may celebrate the role of sensuality and sexuality in our relationship with God.[19] John's contemporary Teresa of Ávila's devotion to God sometimes bordered on the erotic, as we shall in chapter 8.

Poems of Love

It is in poetry that this image is often developed. In the English tradition John Donne (seventeenth century) gives us in his work "Batter My Heart":

> Take me to you, imprison me, for I
> Except you enthral me, never shall be free,
> Nor ever chaste, except you ravish me. (*Holy Sonnets* 140)

And in another of his sonnets he prays:

> And let my amorous soul court thy mild Dove. (18)

Thomas Traherne (1637–74) puts it:

> He did approach, He did me woo;
> I wonder that my God this thing would do.[20]

In hymns, too, we encounter this language. Charles Wesley sings: "Jesus Lover of my soul, let me to thy bosom fly." John Newton's hymn "How Sweet the Name of Jesus Sounds" includes the line: "Jesus! My Shepherd, Husband, Friend."

Nor is this limited to the West. It is universal. In the Orthodox liturgy of the eastern churches Christ is often hailed as "Thou lover of mankind."

Indeed, such terminology, deriving from humanity's most essential dimensions, transcends all religious traditions. In Hinduism, *Bhakti* devotion is offered in the tenderest terms to Krishna. In Islam's Sufi tradition, prayer is considered a "path of love," where the Sufi becomes the "lover" and God the "beloved." This love affair ends only in the ultimate union with the Beloved. This love relationship is depicted in most volumes of Sufi literature and poetry, most famously in the prayers of Persian poet Jalal ad-Dīn Rumi (1207–73):

> I long to sing Your Praises
> but stand mute
> with the agony of wishing in my heart.[21]

Spirituality and Sexuality

As we explore this rich field of metaphor, we inescapably encounter the impact of gender and sexuality on the expressions we use in prayer. Men or gay women may find the idea of falling in love with Jesus or bridal mysticism uncomfortable. Some have worried that this leads to an unbalanced feminization of the church, tracing how for centuries the soul has been depicted as feminine and receptive, but there are recent helpful explorations of feminist approaches to spirituality together with a rediscovery of male spirituality.[22]

Richard Rohr expresses it well when he says:

> What we are searching for in any authentic male or female spirituality is the good and healthy meaning of maleness and femaleness, each being one half of that mystery of God (Gen 1:26-27). Do men approach enlightenment, transformation, conversion and spirituality by a different path to women? Do men and women have different starting points or different symbols that fascinate? My studied opinion is that we do have quite different entrance and "fascination" points, but we nevertheless end up much the same, because the goal is identical—union and even divine union.[67]

Questions for Reflection and Discussion

1. In what circumstances do you consider it appropriate to utilize male imagery in relation to God? When might you use feminine images?

2. What feelings arise in you when you use this sort of language in prayer? What effect does it have on you?

3. How would you describe your relationship with God? What are your primary metaphors?

4. How do you feel about using the language of intimacy with God? Are you comfortable or uncomfortable about this? Why?

5. The sixteenth-century poet Philip Sidney proclaimed, "My true love hath my heart and I have his." For whom might this language be appropriate and for whom might it be inappropriate?

Further Reading

Chittister, Joan D. *Heart of Flesh: A Feminist Spirituality for Women and Men.* Grand Rapids, MI: William B. Eerdmans, 1998.

Jantzen, Grace M. *Power, Gender and Christian Mysticism.* Cambridge Studies in Ideology and Religion. Cambridge: Cambridge University Press, 1995.

Linn, Dennis, Sheila Fabricant, and Matthew Linn. *Good Goats: Healing Our Image of God.* New York: Paulist, 1994.

Llewelyn, Robert. *With Pity Not with Blame: Contemplative Praying with Julian of Norwich & The Cloud of Unknowing.* London: Darton, Longman & Todd, 1982.

McFague, Sallie. *Models of God: Theology for an Ecological, Nuclear Age.* Philadelphia: Fortress, 1987.

Nelson, James B., and Sandra P. Longfellow. *Sexuality and the Sacred: Sources for Theological Reflection.* London: Mowbray, 1994.

Pelphrey, Brant. *Christ our Mother: Julian of Norwich.* London: Darton, Longman & Todd, 1989.

3

The Inspirational Language
of Poets and Artists

Blest pair of Sirens, pledges of
Heaven's joy,
Sphere-born harmonious sisters,
Voice and Verse

—John Milton

The poem or hymn of creation found in the opening lines of Genesis celebrates the goodness of God's world: "The earth brought forth vegetation: plants yielding seed of every kind, and trees of every kind bearing fruit with the seed in it. And God saw that it was good" (Gen 1:12). The psalmist cries out: "the heavens are telling the glory of God" (Ps 19:1). Through the centuries poets and artists communicate spiritual realities through vivid imagery from flora and fauna, discovering natural, horticultural, agricultural, and temporal metaphors for the spiritual life. As Gerald Manley Hopkins puts it:

The world is charged with the grandeur of God.
It will flame out, like shining from shook foil.[1]

William Blake in his poem "Auguries of Innocence" invites us

To see a world in a grain of sand
And a heaven in a wild flower,
Hold infinity in the palm of your hand,
And eternity in an hour.[2]

Troubadour St. Francis of Assisi, the first poet to compose in the Italian vernacular, invites us to recognize and celebrate the radical and essential interconnectedness of all things, displaying a remarkable kinship and sense of unity with creation in his *Canticle of Creation.* He hailed the sun as brother and the moon as sister; he greeted Sister Water and Brother Wind, and in his ministry he approached the fearsome wolf of Gubbio as "brother." At the dawn of capitalism and a creeping consumerist approach to things—Francis was the son of a wealthy cloth-merchant and worked in his shop—he discovered a deep connectedness to all things. Franciscan prayer nurtures such an appreciative, respectful, and nonexploitative approach to the world of nature.[3]

In this chapter we observe how the natural world points to the new creation, especially through the themes of the garden, the greening of the soul, and the growing of the spirit. We see how the seen evokes the unseen and earth points to heaven. We delight in images that organically spring from the world of nature, birds, and animals. We will then conclude by an initial look at the role of art in expressions of spirituality.

The Garden

At the center of the Bible, the rich poem of the Song of Songs invites us to explore two themes in connection with the garden. First, it invites us to enjoy a spontaneous delight in the beauty of creation and to rediscover a sacramental approach to the world.[4] In this Wisdom literature, the garden becomes a meeting place for lovers, place of the tryst, the bride and groom celebrating their love. It resonates with a key life-affirming undercurrent in Jewish spirituality: the goodness and givenness of creation. Indeed, the most typical form of Jewish prayer is the *berakhah*, the blessing of God for his gifts: "Blessed are you, Lord God, King of the universe. . . ." As we noted in chapter two, the sacramentality of creation is celebrated throughout Christian spirituality. In their commentaries on the Song of Songs, writers such as Gregory of Nyssa, Bernard of Clairvaux, and even the Puritan John Owen observe how physicality and materiality point to spirituality: the love of bride and bridegroom speaks of Christ's love for his church.

But the Song of Songs also invites us to a second, darker theme in connection with the garden: the garden emerges as the place not only of personal communion but also as the place of intense struggle. In heartbreak, the bridegroom finds "a garden locked is my sister, my bride" (4:12). Awakening from slumber, the bride finds that her lover has gone: "I sought him, but did not find him; I called to him, but he gave no answer" (5:6). The garden becomes a place of separation, of communion disrupted, of love unrequited. It becomes a place of unanswered questions: "What is your beloved?" (5:9) and "Which way has your beloved turned?" (6:1).

The poem ends with the bride's agonized cry: "O you who dwell in the gardens, my companions are listening for your voice; let me hear it. Make haste, my beloved" (8:13-14).

This double theme, of presence and absence, communion and struggle, alerts us to the ambiguity and paradox of the garden. As a symbol of tenderest communion (God and Adam walk in the garden in the cool of the day), the garden can become a battleground (as Jesus experienced in Gethsemane), while the gardener lingering by the empty tomb (John 20:15) invites us to explore the theme of Eden regained. This is a strong theme in Syriac spirituality: in the Eucharist we taste of Christ, the Tree of Life.

The Greening of Soul

Hildegard of Bingen (1098–1179), poet, mystic, and musician, celebrates our "greening" or *viriditas.* Today we talk about the "greening of the planet," but nine hundred years ago Hildegard celebrated the presence of the Holy Spirit in the created order through the idea of greening: "the earthly expression of the celestial sunlight; greenness is the condition in which earthly beings experience a fulfillment which is both physical and divine; greenness is the blithe overcoming of the dualism between earthly and heavenly."[5] For Hildegard, the wetness or moisture of the planet, revealed in verdant growth, bespeaks the Holy Spirit who "poured out this green freshness of life into the hearts of men and women so that they may bear good fruit."[6] She invites us to see the world differently, overcoming the dichotomy of heaven and earth by glimpsing the heavenly action in the freshness of the planet, mirroring the human soul. We are being summoned from a pragmatic and self-centered consumer mentality, so deeply entrenched in our culture and mindset, to seeing creation as not an entity to be manipulated or exploited but a divine presence to be honored.

Metaphors of Growth

In our spiritual journey, we look to creation for descriptors of the inner, spiritual landscape—what Gerard Manley Hopkins called the *inscape,* the unique characteristics of the soul. The Hebrew Scriptures provide a rich source of imagery here. The prophets, in particular, employ metaphors facing them each day in their very environment:

> Sow for yourselves righteousness; reap steadfast love; break up your fallow ground; for it is time to seek the Lord, that he may come and rain righteousness upon you.

I will be like the dew to Israel; he shall blossom like the lily, he shall strike root like the forests of Lebanon. His shoots shall spread out; his beauty shall be like the olive tree, and his fragrance like that of Lebanon. They shall again live beneath my shadow, they shall flourish as a garden; they shall blossom like the vine, their fragrance shall be like the wine of Lebanon. (Hos 10:12; 14:5-7)

Summoning us into the new creation, Jesus invites us: "Consider the lilies, how they grow" (Luke 12:27). "Consider"—the Greek word means to turn one's attention to, to notice what is happening, or to take a long, slow look. Jesus summons us to a contemplative way of living, a deeply reflective way of seeing the world in which we may learn to see things differently. This sacramental way of viewing reality becomes a dominant theme in the Fourth Gospel. Jesus sees wine, vines, water, bread, sunlight, candlelight, and even shepherding as speaking of himself. The other gospels combine to give us the clear impression that this was an outlook on the world that was truly characteristic of Jesus himself. The secrets of the kingdom reveal themselves through parables of seed, mountain, field, and sea (Matt 13; Mark 11:23).The gospels give us a rich harvest of metaphors: the reign of God germinates as seed in the parables of the sower and the mustard seed; we remember that wheat and tares may grow together (Matt 12–13).

The metaphor about the vine and branches (John 15:1-11) triggers demanding questions that a spiritual director may provide a directee: What is growing well and blossoming, blooming in my spiritual life? Are there buds or potentials that are ready to sprout? Do I notice any dead wood that needs to be taken to the fire and burned? Can I name attitudes or actions that are evidently unproductive and need decisively to be let go of? What parts of my life need pruning in order to let other parts grow and flourish? What sources of inspiration are my spiritual roots exploring? What is watering the soul? Such agrarian imagery invites us to take another look at the root metaphor of growth and fruitfulness, and it encourages us to name and celebrate evidences of spiritual maturity and health. Paul delights in the fruit of the Spirit growing in our lives (Gal 5). He says: "You are God's field" (1 Cor 3:9). He develops agricultural imagery: "The point is this: the one who sows sparingly will also reap sparingly, and the one who sows bountifully will also reap bountifully. . . . He who supplies seed to the sower and bread for food will supply and multiply your seed for sowing and increase the harvest of your righteousness" (2 Cor 9:6, 10).

Seasons of the Spirit

My beloved speaks and says to me:
"Arise, my love, my fair one,
and come away;
for now the winter is past,
the rain is over and gone.
The flowers appear on the earth;
the time of singing has come." (Song of Songs 2:10-12)

We experience periods when our prayer can be described as spiritual springtime: budding, flourishing, blossoming, and fruitfulness. Such themes deriving from the world of nature or agriculture suggest themselves to us now: seeds planted, germinating, and fruiting. But at other times our spiritual experience needs to be depicted in terms of barrenness or dryness, as the English poet-priest George Herbert asks in *The Flower*:

Who would have thought my shrivell'd heart
Could have recovered greenness?

Poet and mystic Evelyn Underhill (1875–1941) images the soul as a tulip bulb placed deep into the earth, as the soul is hidden with Christ in God (Col 3:3). "Go" she says, "with him / Into the dim." It is in the dark that God gives the growth, until it is time to bud and blossom forth: the curtained leaves remind Underhill of "the casement of the heart."[7] This evokes the Easter hymn "Now the green blade riseth from the buried grain," in which seed falls into the ground and dies in order to enable a great harvest (John 12:24):

When our hearts are wintry, grieving, or in pain,
Thy touch can call us back to life again,
Fields of our hearts that dead and bare have been:
Love is come again, like wheat that springeth green.[8]

R. S. Thomas (1913–2000) alludes to a mysterious flower that might represent the experience of prayer:

The soul
grew in me
with its fragrance.
Men came
to me from the four
winds to hear me speak
of the unseen flower by which

I sat, whose roots were not
in the soil, nor its petals the color
of the wide sea; that was
　　　　its own species with its own
　　　　sky over it, shot
with the rainbow of your coming and going.[9]

D. H. Lawrence (1885–1930) in his poem "Shadows" hopes for

　　　　snatches of renewal
　　　　odd, wintry flowers upon the withered stem, yet new, strange
　　　　flowers
　　　　such as my life has not brought forth before, new blossoms
　　　　of me.[10]

"For everything there is a season, and a time for every matter under heaven" (Eccl 3:1). There will be times and seasons in the spiritual life: the winter of the soul gives way to the reenergizing springtime. Temporal metaphors help us celebrate seasons of the spirit; they provide clues with which to read the fecundity or barrenness of the soul. In his poem "Thou Art Indeed Just," Gerard Manley Hopkins prays: "O thou Lord of life, send my roots rain."[11]

As the eighth-century theologian St. John of Damascus puts it in his Easter song:

　　　　All the winter of our sins,
　　　　Long and dark is flying
　　　　From his light. . . .
　　　　Now the queen of seasons, bright
　　　　with the day of splendor.[12]

Day and Night in Christian Spirituality

　　　　Abide with me: fast falls the eventide;
　　　　the darkness deepens; Lord, with me abide:
　　　　when other helpers fail and comforts flee,
　　　　help of the helpless, O abide with me.

These words by Henry Francis Lyte reverberate strongly with those going through the pain of bereavement. The most fundamental metaphors of time, of course, relate to night and day. Blake had written menacingly of "the forests of the night" and Rainer Maria Rilke alludes to the ambiguity of darkness in *Du Dunkelheit*.[13] Night is not necessarily symbolic of death and gloom; it can become positive, since God has a habit of working in the dark, as we will explore in the last chapter.

The eastern tradition of spirituality celebrates the uncreated light of Mt. Tabor—the dazzling healing light of the transfiguration—as a key theme known as the metamorphosis. The Russian theologian Vladimir Lossky comments: "To see the divine light with bodily sight, as the disciples saw it on Mount Tabor, we must participate in and be transformed by it, according to our capacity. Mystical experience implies this change in our nature, its transformation by grace." [14] Dare we enter the divine light—participating in the energies of God—if it might alter us, reshape us, make us different? In the eleventh century St. Simeon the New Theologian offered this prayer to the Holy Spirit:

> You, the gaiety;
> You, the mirth;
> And Your grace, grace of the Spirit of all sanctity,
> Will shine like the sun in all the saints;
> And You, inaccessible sun,
> will shine in their midst
> and all will shine brightly. [15]

Times of transition especially resonate with the shifting states of day. Twilight and dusk, with lengthening shadows and the descent of darkness, may evoke depression or disorientation. With the psalmist we find ourselves yearning for a new dawn: "my soul waits for the Lord more than those who watch for the morning" (130:6). The dispelling of spiritual darkness speaks of resurrection and illumination and evokes the story of Easter: "while it was still dark, Mary Magdalene came to the tomb" (John 20:1). Charles Wesley, in one of his hymns of 1740, powerfully expresses this theme:

> Christ, whose glory fills the skies,
> Christ the true, the only Light,
> Sun of Righteousness, arise!
> Triumph o'er the shades of night:
> Dayspring from on high, be near;
> Daystar, in my heart appear.
>
> Dark and cheerless is the morn
> unaccompanied by thee;
> joyless is the day's return,
> till thy mercy's beams I see,
> till they inward light impart,
> glad my eyes, and warm my heart.

Visit then this soul of mine!
Pierce the gloom of sin and grief!
Fill me, Radiancy Divine;
scatter all my unbelief;
more and more thyself display,
shining to the perfect day.

The Language of Birds

Jesus himself invites us to "look at the birds of the air; they neither sow nor reap nor gather into barns, and yet your heavenly Father feeds them. Are you not of more value than they?" (Matt 6:26). The poets of the Hebrew scriptures developed a rich tradition of expressing spiritual experiences through such imagery. The bird can image the conquering of fears and timidity in its fledgling time of leaving the nest and spreading its wings. We are given the vivid image of a parent eagle rousing chicks in order to get them out of the coziness of the nest:

Just as an eagle stirs up its nest, encouraging its young to fly,
and then hovers over them in case they need help,
And spreads its wings and catches them if they fall,
and carries them up high on its wings
So the Eternal guided Jacob through the wilderness
without the help of any foreign god. (Deut 32:11-12, *The Voice*)

Another great bird describes the Exodus experience and becomes a re-peated motif for deliverance and salvation: "You have seen what I did to the Egyptians, and how I bore you on eagles' wings and brought you to myself" (Exod 19:4). But if God is an eagle, so his people can likewise fly in confidence:

but those who wait for the LORD shall renew their strength,
they shall mount up with wings like eagles,
they shall run and not be weary,
they shall walk and not faint. (Isa 40:31)

However, the bird can represent vulnerability and the experience of ex-posure to danger:

Like fluttering birds, like scattered nestlings,
so are the daughters of Moab at the fords of the Arnon. (Isa 16:2)

The Common English Bible translates this:

> The daughters of Moab at the fords of the Arnon are like orphaned
> birds pushed from the nest. (CEB)

The psalmist expresses very personal feelings of abandonment and
desolation:

> I am like an owl of the wilderness,
>   like a little owl of the waste places.
> I lie awake;
>   I am like a lonely bird on the housetop. (Ps 102:6, 7)

Yet he can take solace in the homing instinct of the bird, its sense of belonging and homecoming:

> Even the sparrow finds a home,
>   and the swallow a nest for herself,
>   where she may lay her young,
> at your altars, O LORD of hosts,
>   my King and my God. (Ps 84:3)

The psalms look to the birds for metaphors of captivity and freedom:

> We have escaped like a bird
>   from the snare of the fowlers;
> the snare is broken,
>   and we have escaped. (Ps 124:7)

> And I say, "O that I had wings like a dove!
>   I would fly away and be at rest. (Ps 55:6)

Birds in flight become a graceful metaphor for a sense of release from
being trapped. We may have the fragility of the dove and but also, at times,
the confidence of the eagle!

Animal Images of the Experience of God

Since the second century, Christians have been involved in forming documents called bestiaries, which celebrated the range of creatures in the world.
Even some early church fathers like Augustine, Ambrose, and Gregory
the Great used illustrations from the bestiaries in their preaching, while
Christian artists drew inspiration from these sources for their pictorial
compositions. Decorations based on the bestiaries have been found as early
as the second-century catacombs in Rome. Animals appeared in the mosaic
art of the early churches, and later in stonework and stained glass windows.

Biblical writers employed animal imagery to convey and express the experience both of the judgment and the tenderness of God. He is both the lion and the lamb. Hosea declares: "The lion has roared; who will not fear? The Lord God has spoken" (3:8). Recounting "salvation history" he conveys not only the experience of divine provision but also, in shocking terms, the terror of being devoured and attacked by God:

> Yet I have been the Lord your God ever since the land of Egypt; you know no God but me, and besides me there is no savior. It was I who fed you in the wilderness, in the land of drought. When I fed them, they were satisfied; they were satisfied, and their heart was proud; therefore they forgot me. So I will become like a lion to them, like a leopard I will lurk beside the way. I will fall upon them like a bear robbed of her cubs, and will tear open the covering of their heart; there I will devour them like a lion, as a wild animal would mangle them. (Hos 13:4-8)

But the lion image can also communicate the majestic nature of Christ: "Do not weep. See, the Lion of the tribe of Judah, the Root of David, has conquered" (Rev 5:5). The Bible also uses the lion symbol to sometimes describe Satan as one going around and seeking prey (1 Pet 5:8).

Balancing such menacing imagery, Jesus is also depicted as a lamb. John the Baptist hails Jesus as "the lamb of God" (John 1:29, 36), and this is also taken up in the book of Revelation: "Then I saw . . . a Lamb standing as if it had been slaughtered" (5:6). The author of 1 Peter says that we have been redeemed "with the precious blood of Christ, like that of a lamb without defect or blemish" (1 Pet 1:19).

Animal Images of Human Behavior

We too can feel vulnerability as if we are being sent out "as lambs in the midst of wolves" (Luke 10:3). A range of animals expresses our self-understanding. One may be like a graceful deer, beautiful and swift, one of the most gracious and fastest wild animals in the Bible. Psalm 18:33 says: "He makes my feet like the feet of a deer; he enables me to stand on the heights." The beloved cries out:

> Until the day breathes and the shadows flee,
> turn, my beloved, be like a gazelle or a young stag on the cleft
> mountains. (Song 2:17)

The psalmist memorably sings:

> As a deer longs for flowing streams,
> so my soul longs for you, O God. (Ps 42:1; see also Isa 35:6; Ps 18:32)

But the psalms also report an experience that feels like being hounded by a pack of ferocious dogs:

> Dogs have surrounded me;
> a band of evil men has encircled me. (Ps 22:16)

Among the prophets, Hosea celebrates the covenant relationship in terms of a farmer with domesticated or tamed animals: "Ephraim was a trained heifer" (10:11). God's people, however, turn wild: "Like a stubborn heifer, Israel is stubborn; can the Lord now feed them like a lamb in a broad pasture?" (4:16). As it were, we break out of the enclosure and place ourselves in a place of danger, where we can be ravaged by wild beasts, until we return to the discipline and care of the master. A recent example of such animal imagery is afforded by approaches to the Enneagram tool for prayer. Are you in prayer a terrier, a cat, a peacock, a monkey, a rhinoceros, or an elephant? [16]

The Scriptures abound with insect imagery too. St Francis de Sales delighted in natural metaphors, and his *Introduction to the Devout Life* contains rich seams to mine, with its many examples of spiritual direction:

> True devotion never causes harm, but rather perfects everything we do . . . the bee sucks honey from the flowers without harming them, leaving them as whole and fresh as when it found them. Devotion goes further, not only is it unharmful to any state of life, it adorns and beautifies it. . . . As the mouth of the bee is only used for honey, so should your tongue be ever honeyed as it were, with God, while you are never more happy than when you have his praises on your lips.[17]

The Language of Artists

Consider the words of Nick Holtam, when vicar of London's St. Martin-in-the-Fields, a church with a rich tradition of participation in and patronage of the arts:

> Most of us can find worth and meaning in art. People often speak of losing themselves in a painting or a work of art, preoccupied by something or someone beyond the self . . . in losing our self-centered selves we find ourselves in relation to one another, the wide earth and the creator. It happens in an art gallery as it does in church.[18]

A picture paints a thousand words. As a powerful medium in the communication of spiritual realities, art can play a creative role in our spiritual lives. It is not the purpose of art to be liked or admired, but to hearten, inspire, and disturb. It does not aim to answer questions but to raise them, provoke, invoke, and evoke.

We can use paintings and art in perhaps three different ways in our life of prayer. First, we can allow a picture to take us into prayer, to transport us, to be a vehicle for bringing us into the deeper reaches of prayer. Art invites us to contemplate, to gaze, to look closely at details, to learn the art of attentiveness. It invites us to enter someone else's world and to appreciate one's worldview and way of interpreting reality.

Second, as we look at a painting we realize that it equips us to speak of our own inner lives. It suggests images and vocabulary enabling us to become more articulate about our relationship with God: symbols and depictions may reverberate and resonate with where we're at, or where we want to go.

Third, it may inspire us to express ourselves creatively, attempting to paint or draw or make something. There are resources available to help us.[19] The practice of art can help us explore inner themes and express inner longings that words cannot communicate.

One of the functions of art is that it communicates feelings and emotions as well as ideas and thoughts. Leo Tolstoy (1828–1910) put it in his essay "What is Art?": "To evoke in oneself a feeling one has once experienced and having evoked it in oneself then by means of movements, lines, colors, sounds or forms expressed in words, so to transmit this feeling that others experience the same thing—this is the activity of art.[20]

As art communicates feelings, it also interprets and finds meaning in them, and so it becomes a means of perception and comprehension. In his book *Languages of Art*, Nelson Goodman, for example, explores how through different media and a range of symbols, art may have a cognitive role in our lives and help us to see and understand experience differently. Thus art can have a valuable role to play in spiritual direction and in the expression of inner experience of the divine, externalizing the interiority and expressing on canvas or in sculpture the invisible realities of prayer. Art may sometimes enable an unlocking: "the work of art is in some sense a liberation of the personality; normally our feelings are inhibited and repressed. We contemplate a work of art, and immediately there is a release . . . art is a release, but it is also a bracing."[21] The millennium exhibition at the National Gallery, *Seeing Salvation*, opened many people's eyes to fresh perceptions of Jesus of Nazareth.[22] Art draws us to the very edge of mystery.

This prompts us to see our store of images as a paintbox and to reflect on the color of our prayer. Bruce Duncan introduces us to the range of praying styles according to Jungian typology: blue prayer, for example, is spacious and reflective thinking prayer, while red prayer is passionate, sensuous, and intercessory.[23] We noted above Hildegard of Bingen's greening of the soul. John Donne wrote in the fourth of his "Holy Sonnets":

> O my black soul!
> . . . O make thyself with holy mourning black,
> And red with blushing, as thou art with sin;
> Or wash thee in Christ's blood, which hath this might,
> That being red, it dyes red souls to white.

What is the color of your prayer? What is the color of the soul?

Questions for Reflection and Discussion

1. How would you describe the season of life in which you find yourself?

2. What are the signs of spiritual growth? How do you celebrate your spiritual fruitfulness?

3. Are there things that are impeding growth or reducing your harvest?

4. In what ways does your soul shimmer?

5. What animal or bird most closely resembles your spiritual experience right now?

Further Reading

Dreyer, Elizabeth A. *Holy Power, Holy Presence: Rediscovering Medieval Metaphors for the Holy Spirit.* Mahwah, NJ: Paulist Press, 2007.

Stanley, Bruce. *Forest Church: A Field Guide to Nature Connection for Groups and Individuals.* Llangurig, Powys: Mystic Christ, 2003.

4

The Invigorating Language of Singers and Dancers

My heart is steadfast, O God,
my heart is steadfast;
I will sing and make melody.
Awake, my soul!
Awake, O harp and lyre!
I will awake the dawn.

—Ps 108:1-2

Language of Singers

Music has been called "the language of the soul." The Bible opens with an ancient Hebrew hymn of praise and closes with a book that incorporates many hymns from the worship of the first Christians.[1] They are presented as the songs of heaven. At the center of the Scriptures lies the hymnbook of the temple, the Psalter, which is always beseeching us to express ourselves in song:

Sing to the Lord a new song. (Ps 96:1)

Clap your hands, all you peoples;
    shout to God with loud songs of joy. (Ps 47:1)
Raise a song, sound the tambourine,
    the sweet lyre with the harp. (Ps 81:2)

The gospels—especially Luke, which opens with the songs of Mary (*Magnificat*), Zechariah (*Benedictus*), and Simeon (*Nunc Dimmittis*), and moves swiftly to the song of the angels—resound with song. Indeed, the biblical scholar Raymond Brown believed that these are the songs of the *anawim*, the poor members of the impoverished church of Jerusalem.[2]

The letter to the Colossians exhorts us: "Let the word of Christ dwell in you richly; teach and admonish one another in all wisdom; and with gratitude in your hearts sing psalms, hymns, and spiritual songs to God" (3:16). Paul's own advice is: "I will sing praise with the spirit, but I will sing praise with the mind also. . . . When you come together, each one has a hymn, a lesson, a revelation, a tongue, or an interpretation. Let all things be done for building up" (1 Cor 14:15, 26). Paul's singing in the prison in Philippi triggered an earthquake! (Acts 16:25).

Hymns and Songs in Prayer and Spiritual Direction

St. Augustine is reputed to have said that the one who sings prays twice. He cried out: "We are an Easter people and Alleluia is our song!" After the great songs in Luke's gospel, the Christian tradition of hymnody continues in the New Testament with Philippians 2:6-11 and flourishes in the exultant songs preserved in the book of Revelation.[3] Ephrem the Syrian provides a stunning collection of songs in the fourth century. Hymn writers have inspired prayer in every generation, from Wesley to Kendrick.[4]

How can hymns and songs be used in spiritual direction? We engage with the psalms when we take on our own lips the cries from the heart, the raw expressions of grief, confusion, or penitence. Plugging in, as it were, to the spiritual movements expressed in the psalms, we can move from distress to new hope and confidence: such psalms as 6, 13, 22, 35, 42, 73, and 102 stimulate and encourage spiritual transitions or shifts taking place in our own times of prayer.

In the same way, one can make one's own an experiential hymn that speaks to one's condition, like Newton's "Amazing Grace" or William Cowper's 1772 hymn:

> O for a closer walk with God,
> a calm and heavenly frame,
> a light to shine upon the road
> that leads me to the Lamb!
>
> Where is the blessedness I knew
> when first I saw the Lord?
> Where is the soul-refreshing view
> of Jesus and his word?
>
> Return, O holy Dove, return,
> sweet messenger of rest;

I hate the sins that made thee mourn,
and drove thee from my breast.

One may compose a new song to the Lord, taking as a model the *Magnificat*, which delights in what God is doing in one's life. Song and poetry seem to arise authentically from our depths and are excellent examples of "primary speech" springing straight from the soul.[5] There is a certain immediacy in song and hymnwriting that gives voice to the invisible realities of the human spirit.

Jesus the Dancer

Dance then wherever you may be
I am the Lord of the Dance, said he[6]

We often forget that originally carols were sung to accompany dances, and carols have been written celebrating Jesus the dancer. John Gardner famously composed his carol "Tomorrow Shall Be My Dancing Day" by adapting a medieval original. It is written in the first person because it portrays Jesus speaking on the night before his conception, envisioning his unfolding ministry as a dance with his bride, the church.[7] Here Jesus' vocation is "To call my true love to my dance." In fact, Jesus does allude to himself in the gospels as the leader of a dance, both physical and metaphorical. A saying tucked away in Matthew 11:7 sums up Jesus' exhilaration and exasperation: "But to what will I compare this generation? It is like children sitting in the marketplaces and calling to one another: 'We played the flute for you and you did not dance.'" Jesus is dismayed with the people's unresponsiveness—they simply will not join in the dance. I can imagine Jesus also phrasing this positively: "The Kingdom is at hand. Listen to the children! As they are piping, they call out: 'Come and join in the dance!'"

This dance language appears in other places on the lips of Jesus. In the Beatitudes Jesus says: "Blessed are you when people hate you, and when they exclude you . . . on account of the Son of Man. Rejoice in that day and dance for joy, for surely your reward is great in heaven" (Luke 6:22-23). Jesus calls his disciples to dance for joy in the very hour that they are persecuted. The dance is to be the response to pain. This Beatitude is an echo of Psalm 30: "You have turned my mourning into dancing; you have taken off my sackcloth and clothed me with joy" (v. 11). In the great parable of the Prodigal Son, the symbol of the kingdom of God, the expression of the father's joy at the return of the wayward son is precisely the dance: the elder son, coming in from the field, hears music and dancing (Luke 15:25).

Join the Dance

Dancing is a recurrent theme in the Hebrew Scriptures. The prophet Zephaniah celebrates God's love in this image:

> He will exult with joy over you,
> he will renew you by his love;
> he will dance with shouts of joy for you
> as on a day of festival. (Zeph 3:17, Jerusalem Bible)

The psalms call upon us repeatedly to dance. Psalm 149:2-3 cries out to the people:

> Let Israel be glad in its Maker;
>   let the children of Zion rejoice in their King.
> Let them praise his name with dancing,
>   making melody to him with tambourine and lyre.

Psalm 150 exhorts us: "Praise him with lute and harp! Praise him with tambourine and dance!" (vv. 3-4). Celebrating Jerusalem as the symbolic birthplace of all peoples, Psalm 87 declares: "Singers and dancers alike say, 'All my springs are in you.'" Indeed, it is probable that some of the psalms were written as dances or at least to accompany exuberant liturgical processions:

"Clap your hands, all you peoples; shout to God with loud songs of joy" (Ps 47:1). Psalm 114:6 speaks of the mountains skipping or dancing like rams. *The Message* gives dramatic translations:

> God's thunder sets the oak trees dancing
> A wild dance, whirling . . .
> We fall to our knees—we call out, "Glory!" (Ps 29:9, *The Message*).
> Oh, visit the earth, ask her to join the dance! (Ps 65:9, *The Message*).
>
> You did it: you changed wild lament into whirling dance;
> You ripped off my black mourning band and decked me with
>   wildflowers.
> I'm about to burst with song; I can't keep quiet about you.
>   (Ps 30:11-12, *The Message*)

Dancing in the Prophets

In the prophets, the dance becomes a metaphor for salvation and a symbol of messianic hope. In his great chapter on the new covenant Jeremiah writes:

Again I will build you, and you shall be built,
  O virgin Israel!
Again you shall take your tambourines,
  and go forth in the dance of the merrymakers. . . .
Then shall the young women rejoice in the dance,
  And the young men and the old shall be merry.
I will turn their mourning into joy,
  I will comfort them, and give them gladness for sorrow. (Jer 31:4, 13)

Isaiah gives this vivid image of redemption: "For you shall go out in joy, and be led back in peace; the mountains and the hills before you shall burst into song, and all the trees of field clap their hands" (Isa 55:12).

Dancing in the New Testament

In the gospels, even the dour John the Baptist dances, albeit in the womb: "Elizabeth exclaims, at Mary's visit to her, 'As soon as the sound of your greeting reached my ears, the baby in my womb leaped for joy'" (Luke 1:44). In the Acts of the Apostles, dance follows healing: the lame man, when cured, is unstoppable: "Jumping up, he stood and began to walk, and he entered the temple with them, walking and leaping and praising God" (Acts 3:8). This is the dance of praise, the dance of salvation: the people were filled with amazement and wonder. So, in the Scriptures, we see dance as an expression of worship and joy, a sign or sacrament of salvation.

We need to reconceive the image of Jesus and reimagine him: see him as leading the dance of his disciples. In the second century Acts of John, a book that was not included in the canon of the New Testament, celebrates how Jesus led his disciples in "a round dance of the cross" at the Last Supper:

Jesus told us to form in a circle and hold each others' hands, and he
  himself stood
in the middle, and said, "Respond to me with 'Amen.'"
So he began by singing a hymn and declaring,
  "Glory to you, Father."
And we circled around him and responded to him,
  "Amen."
  "Glory to you, Word. Glory to you, grace."
  "Amen."
  "Glory to you, Spirit. Glory to you holy one. Glory to your glory"
  "Amen"[8]

It is not so difficult to see Jesus as a dancer and choreographer of the kingdom. With a twinkle in his eye, he looks at us and says: "Why stay sitting at the sidelines? Join in the dance of the kingdom!" As Thomas Merton puts it:

> The Lord plays and diverts Himself in the garden of His creation, and if we could let go of our own obsession with what we think is the meaning of it all, we might be able to hear His call and follow Him in His mysterious, cosmic dance. . . .
>
> For the world and time are the dance of the Lord in emptiness. The silence of the spheres is the music of a wedding feast. . . . Indeed, we are in the midst of it, and it is in the midst of us, for it beats in our very blood, whether we want it to or not.
>
> Yet the fact remains that we are invited to forget ourselves on purpose, cast our awful solemnity to the winds and join in the general dance.[9]

The Dance of Prayer

This is a dynamic and energizing metaphor of prayer, sensual, and incarnational. The role of the spiritual director is to support the dance of the kingdom. He or she must first summon and invite others to the dance. The director has a role to help in the shaping of the choreography and will have clarified to herself or himself some idea of where the dance is going. This is not set in stone but rather must be fluid and capable of revision, if one stays open to God and the needs of others. But a folk dance needs a caller, one who will give clear and audible instructions and directions. Our role as spiritual directors is to open up a space where people can be free and also learn to share disciplines. Three imperatives suggest themselves.

1. In Sync with God's Spirit

"Let's keep each step in perfect sync with God's Spirit." This is the Voice translation's rendition of Paul's striking phrase from Galatians 5:25; the New International Version reads: "Let us keep in step with the Spirit" (NIV). We are called to go with the flow of the Spirit, to get in tune with God, to stay in step, to discern the rhythms of God's dance, the dance of the universe, and to attain a synchronicity with the divine. In Christian theology, the dynamic relation between the persons of the Trinity was described by St. Basil in the fourth century as a dance or *perichoresis*. This conveys something of the reciprocal, mutual indwelling of Father, Son, and Holy Spirit. As the idea developed, it communicated the idea that humanity is called to participate in an ever-creative dance of the Trinity. The Trinity is not a dogma or idea; the Trinity is a dance to be joined! As Baxter Kruger puts it:

Before the universe came to be, before the heavens were called forth with stars and moons, before the earth was carved in infinite beauty and human life was fashioned with style and grace and glory, before there was anything, there was the great dance of life shared by the Father, Son and Spirit. In staggering and lavish love, this God determined to open the circle and share the Trinitarian life with others. As an act of mind-boggling and astounding philanthropy, the Father, Son and Spirit chose to create human beings and share the great dance with them.[10]

Kruger suggests that the great dance becomes humanity's greatest puzzle:

In one way or another, aren't we all after the great dance? Is that not the story of our lives, our deepest longing? To my mind, the central passion of the human heart is to be filled with the great dance, and the chief and maddening riddle of human life is to understand what the dance is and how to live in it.[11]

We are summoned to enter the very energy and dynamic of God! As Jude 1:21 puts it: "And keep in step with God's love, as you wait for our Lord Jesus Christ to show how kind he is by giving you eternal life" (CEV). Elizabeth Johnson writes of the dance of ministry: "Dancers whirl and intertwine in unusual patterns; the floor is circled in seemingly chaotic ways; rhythms are diverse. . . . Resolution is achieved unexpectedly. Music, light and shadow, color and wonderfully supple motion coalesce in dancing that is not smoothly predicable and repetitive, as is a round dance, and yet it is just as highly disciplined. Its order is more complex."[12]

The concept of the Trinity's *perichoresis* is, of course, beautifully and movingly depicted in the fifteenth-century icon of the Trinity by Andrei Rublev. It depicts the Trinity as three angels around a table in a poise of mutual respect and reciprocal love. I had always imagined this famous icon to be about a foot square and had seen countless reproductions. When I saw the original recently in the Tretyakov Gallery in Moscow I was completely taken aback. It is about six feet square and the gap at the front, between the angels, is precisely the size of a human person: the viewer of the icon, standing in front of it, finds himself or herself dancing with the Trinity! The space at the front of the icon invites the viewer to step into God's circular dance and become a participant, not an observer. As Leonardo Boff puts it: "This union–communion–perichoresis opens outwards: invites human beings and the whole universe to insert themselves in the divine life."[13] C. S. Lewis affirms:

> the most important difference between Christianity and all other
> religions [is this]: that in Christianity God is not a static thing . . . but
> a dynamic, pulsating activity, a life, almost a kind of drama. Almost,
> if you will not think me irreverent, a kind of dance. . . . The whole
> dance, or drama, or pattern of this three-Personal life is to be played
> out in each one of us: or (putting it the other way around) each one
> of us has got to enter that pattern, take his place in that dance. There
> is no other way to the happiness for which we are made.[14]

The spiritual director must ensure that even the clumsy and left-footed
have a treasured place in the circle of prayer. This will require people to
leave their comfort zones and not stay, like the sour elder brother in the
parable of the Prodigal Son, on the outside looking in. The spiritual director
will always be alert to those who want to stay on the sidelines. He or she will
encourage others toward greater trust and risk, especially when dancers
are required to find a partner to dance with. We have to learn to trust the
partner, even if we do not know him or her well. The spiritual director will
also be aware that a certain self-forgetfulness is required of all; directors
leave aside their own agendas for the sake of the community dance.

We invite them to dance to the music of the Spirit. We are inviting them
to gently explore the movement of the Spirit. As Paul reminds us, there is
a space for everyone (1 Cor 12); all gifts are welcome. As Henri Nouwen
puts it: "That is the great and wonderful mystery of God becoming flesh to
live among us. God . . . invites us to learn to dance—not alone, but with
others, sharing in God's own compassion, as we both give and receive it." [15]

2. Let Go and Loosen Up

In his book *Turn my Mourning into Dancing*, Henri Nouwen affirms that
God calls us from holding tight to things in a spirit of control to loosening
our grip on things:

> How can we live with greater willingness to let go? Another step
> in turning our mourning into dancing has to do with not clutching
> what we have . . . not trying to choreograph our own or others' lives,
> but to surrender to the God whom we love and want to follow. God
> invites us to experience our not being in control as an invitation to
> faith . . . our tight grip on life—its joys and even its sorrows—can
> loosen. We too can learn again to fly—to dance.[16]

Something happens when we relax our grip. "Mourning opens us to a
future we could not imagine on our own—one that includes a dance. . . .

For even while we mourn, we do not forget how our life can ultimately join God's larger dance of life and hope." [17]

We are also invited by God in his dance to loosen up. Participants in a community dance are invited to catch the joy and allow themselves to smile and laugh. Mistakes will be made, and we bear with one another graciously and with big humor. We learn to discard our serious self-consciousness. We accept each other; we are energized. The spiritual director realizes that this image resonates with that of the fool or the clown. We find that the joy of the dance is contagious, infectious, and life-affirming. Saint John of Damascus links dancing with sheer delight in God:

> You have cast a spell of longing over me, O Christ,
> And changed me with your divine yearning;
> . . . make me worthy to be filled with delight in you,
> That, dancing, I may magnify your two comings,
> O Good One. [18]

Paul puts it in 1 Thessalonians 4:1-3 : "One final word, friends. We ask you—*urge* is more like it—that you keep on doing what we told you to do to please God, not in a dogged religious plod, but in a living, spirited dance" (*The Message*). And contemplative poet Ann Lewin prays:

> Flame-dancing Spirit, come,
> Sweep us off our feet and
> Dance us through our days.
> Surprise us with your rhythms,
> Dare us to try new steps, explore
> New patterns and new partnerships.
> Release us from old routines
> To swing in abandoned joy
> And fearful adventure.
> And in the intervals,
> Rest us,
> In your still centre. [19]

3. Dance in the Streets

The musician John Fischer writes:

> The Spirit of God dances. He can't be tamed. He won't be contained. He refuses to be confined to a weekend retreat, an evening meeting, or even a moment of devotion . . . the Spirit of God dances out into the streets. He dances by the harlots in the red-light districts,

by the victims of AIDS in lonely homes, by bag ladies in the inner cities. . . . He finds the orphans and widows and dances through the lonely pain of their lives

But is not only the Spirit of God who dances on the streets.

Well, here I am. I'm out on the floor again and I can hear the music starting up. Great! I think I'm finally ready to dance. But wait a minute . . . this isn't a floor; it's asphalt. Good grief, we're out on the street!

Oh no, I don't think I signed up for this. I thought this was going to be a nice, controlled Christian dance in the church gymnasium. . . . Somebody turned my nice, safe party out onto the streets. . . . This isn't safe; this definitely is not safe. I thought this was going to be an entirely different dance.[20]

God leads our dance into the market places. That is where the children were located: "this generation is like children sitting in the marketplaces and calling to one another . . . 'We played the flute for you and you did not dance'" (Matt 11:17). We are not invited to a cozy barn dance in the church hall but to risky witness and care in the community. I picture Jesus, setting the rhythm and creating the route, leading a conga line through our town, little groups breaking off to minister and care as we pass the hurting and down-and-out. Jesus energizes us for a dance that takes us to the streets!

Jesus, Lord of the Dance?

Sydney Carter wrote this now-classic hymn in 1963 and published it in 1967. He described it as a carol, "a dancing kind of song, the life of which is in the dance as much as in the verbal statement." He adapted the tune from a song sung by the Quaker community; it quickly became one of the top five songs sung in British school assembles, and it was included in *Common Praise*, a revision of the Church of England's *Hymns Ancient and Modern*.

Carter related his surprise at the popularity of the song: "I did not think the churches would like it at all. I thought many people would find it pretty far flown, probably heretical and anyway dubiously Christian. But in fact people did sing it and, unknown to me, it touched a chord. . . . Anyway, it's the sort of Christianity I believe in." Carter goes on to share his view of the person of Christ: "I see Christ as the incarnation of the piper who is calling us. He dances that shape and pattern which is at the heart of our reality. . . . I sing of the dancing pattern in the life and words of Jesus. Whether Jesus ever leaped in Galilee to the rhythm of a pipe or drum I do not know. We are told that David danced (and as an act of worship too), so it is not impossible."[21]

They cut me down
And I leapt up high;
I am the life
That'll never, never die;
I'll live in you
If you'll live in me—
I am the Lord
Of the Dance, said he.
> And I'll lead you all, wherever you may be,
> And I'll lead you all in the Dance, said he.

Questions for Reflection and Discussion

1. Synchronicity, mutuality, reciprocity: which do you find the greatest challenge in your spiritual life (1 Cor 12)?

2. What does your prayer or ministry look like if reconceived or reimagined as a dance? In what ways is the Christian to be dancer, choreographer, conductor, or piper?

3. What is holding you back from dancing with Christ more freely? Name your fears and insecurities and hesitations—and drop them onto the dancefloor, treading them underfoot!

4. John Donne wrote: "I shall be made thy Music; As I come/I tune the Instrument here at the door" ("Hymn to God my God, In My Sickness"). What instrument will you be for God? What is the character of the music of your prayer?

5. How do you find yourself responding to the prayer:

   > What do you want of me, Lord?
   > Where do you want me to serve you?
   > Where can I sing your praises ?
   > I am Your Song. . . .

   > I hear you call my name, Lord,
   > and I am moved within me.
   > Your Spirit stirs my deepest self,
   > Sing your songs in me.[22]

Further Reading

Greenwood, Robin. *Practising Community: The Task of the Local Church.* London: SPCK, 1996.

Lonsdale, David. *Listening to the Music of the Spirit: The Art of Discernment.* South Bend, IN: Ave Maria, 1992.

Mayne, Michael. *Learning to Dance.* London: Darton, Longman & Todd, 2001.

Walling, Jeff. *Daring to Dance with God: Stepping into God's Embrace.* Los Angeles: Howard, 2000.

5

The Energizing Language of Pilgrims and Travelers

All the paths of the Lord are
steadfast love and faithfulness.

−Ps 24:4

The life of discipleship is a constant dance between movement and stillness. We are called to be contemplatives in action—people on the move, but holding in our hearts a center of quietude. The spiritual life is worked out within the interplay between stability and rootedness on the one hand and, on the other, the dynamic call to progress and move on. The Christian experience can be described as a pilgrimage, an adventure, a voyage, a quest, an odyssey, or a spiritual walk with God. Here we explore the biblical background to this imagery and its use in Christian spirituality.[1]

The Metaphor of the Spiritual Journey

Biblical writers utilize the image of the pathway or road as a metaphor for entering upon God's way of justice and salvation. Psalm 24 prays for guidance:

> Make me to know your ways, O Lord;
>   Teach me your paths. . . .
> He leads the humble in what is right,
>   And teaches the humble his way.

The prophet Isaiah envisions a path to redemption: "A highway will be there, and it shall be called the Holy Way; the unclean shall not travel on it, but it shall be for God's people; no traveler, not even fools, shall go astray

. . . but the redeemed shall walk there. And the ransomed of the Lord shall return, and come to Zion with singing" (Isa 35:8-10). The prophet hopes for the people's return from their exile, and sees the bleak desert becoming a "road of holiness" and a new exodus journey toward freedom.

This imagery is echoed in the vision that is taken up by John the Baptist: "As it is written in the words of the prophet Isaiah, 'The voice of one crying out in the wilderness: "prepare the way of the Lord, make his paths straight. Every valley shall be filled, and every mountain and hill shall be made low, and the crooked shall be made straight, and the rough places made smooth; and all flesh shall see the salvation of God"'" (Luke 3:3-6; cf. John 1:23). The Baptist identifies closely with the landscape. As he looks out on the wild and precipitous cliffs and escarpments of the Judean wilderness, he can envision with Isaiah a leveling of the impossible natural barriers and the raising of new pathways to freedom. What was impassable and impenetrable becomes a gateway to a new future for God's people. John's message is that we need to open up entry-points for the coming Messiah in the landscape of our lives.

A major theme in Mark's gospel is following Jesus along an unpredictable road: "They were on the road, going up to Jerusalem, and Jesus was walking ahead of them; they were amazed" (Mark 10:32). The first Christians were called in the Acts of the Apostles the "followers of the Way." Paul develops his view of the Christian life in terms of a race to be run (Phil 3:12-15; see also 2 Tim 2:5; 4:7-8); we are called to be spiritual athletes, familiar with *ascesis* or training. Paul loves the metaphor of moving forward (Gal 5:16). Such a theme, of course, has been celebrated through the centuries. We recall John Bunyan's *Pilgrim's Progress* written in the seventeenth century, and we will discover that this is a theme that resonates with every century of Christian experience. In the course of his trek, Christian is greeted by Goodwill, who says to him:

> We do not reject any who come. No matter what they have done before coming, they are in no wise cast out. And now, my good pilgrim, come with me a little way, and I will show you the way to go. Now look yonder. Do you see that narrow way? That is the road you must take. It was travelled by the patriarchs in olden times, and by the prophets, and by Christ and His apostles; and it is as straight as a line can make it.[2]

Christian asks him: "But are there no turnings or windings by which a stranger may lose his way?" Goodwill responds: "Yes, there are many roads branching off from this one, but you can distinguish the right way from the wrong, for the right way is the only road that is straight and narrow."[3] Maybe the spiritual life is not so easy as this, but the imagery of the journey gives us a rich vocabulary with which to describe key features in the spiritual adventure. Seven themes predominate: exile and homecoming; traveling into freedom; passing through storms and chaos; voyaging into the deep; overcoming barriers; the need for maps; and navigating multiple directions.

Exile and Homecoming

The Garden of Eden is the primordial image of communion of God, where Adam walks with God in the cool of the day. The exclusion from the garden resonates with our self-imposed exile from God due to our own personal choices, which shatter and fragment the experience of communion with God. There is a nostalgia and longing to return to Eden: it becomes a symbol of a paradise lost that can be regained, as Ezekiel 36: 34-35 depicts: "The land that was desolate shall be tilled, instead of being the desolation that it was in the sight of all who passed by. And they will say, 'This land that was desolate has become like the garden of Eden.'"

Isaiah expresses humanity's longing to return to things as they should be: "For the Lord will comfort Zion; he will comfort all her waste places, and will make her wilderness like Eden, her desert like the garden of the Lord; joy and gladness will be found in her, thanksgiving and the voice of song" (Isa 51:3).

In his poem "One Foot in Eden" Edwin Muir celebrates Eden as a place of hope:

> Yet still from Eden springs the root
> As clean as on the starting day.[4]

In a different vein, Abraham is the archetypal pilgrim figure: "Now the LORD said to Abram, "Go from your country and your kindred and your father's house to the land that I will show you" (Gen 12:1). God calls him to leave his usual security zone, even his place of residence, and take to the road, even though the destination is undisclosed. The letter to the Hebrews celebrates Abraham and Sarah's pilgrim status: "They confessed that they were strangers and foreigners on the earth, for people who speak in this way make it clear that they are seeking a homeland." (Heb 11:13-14).

This resonates with our experience of quitting our comfort zone and venturing forth in the journey of faith. We might find ourselves identifying with the prodigal son, for that parable expresses the human experience of lostness, dislocation, and confusion. We feel at a distance from God, as if we were in a "far country." There are times in the spiritual life when we feel adrift, when we become intensely aware of our ache for God, our longing for God. This echoes the Jewish theme of *galut,* or exile.[5] Like refugees of old we can say:

> By the rivers of Babylon—
>   there we sat down and there we wept
> On the willows there we hung up our harps.
> For there our captors asked us for songs
>   "Sing us one of the songs of Zion!"
> How could we sing the LORD's song in a foreign land? (Ps 137:1-3)

Like the prodigal we "come to our senses" and the experience of returning to God becomes a homecoming, a fundamental sense of reconnecting with our origins, the source of our life.

But we know, deep down, that we do not belong to this earth. We are only passing through: "our homeland is in heaven" (Phil 3:20, NCV). We declare, with the letter to the Hebrews: "For here we have no lasting city, but we are looking for the city that is to come" (Heb 13:14).

Journey into Freedom

The primordial journey of the people of God is across the Red Sea, prefiguring the experience of baptism. As in the story of Noah, the waters of destruction and judgment become the place of salvation (1 Pet 3:20-21), so God also saves his people through waters—as he led the people of Israel to freedom across the Red Sea—parted by Moses.

Jesus came through deep and terrifying waters of death to new life, so the first Christians were baptized in the river or the sea, going down under the water drowning their sins and rising up out of the water to newness of life. This passage through the waters marks the beginning of the spiritual journey. As a baptismal rite puts it: "Through the deep waters of death you brought your Son, and raised him to life in triumph. . . . We thank you, Father, for the water of Baptism: in it we are buried with Christ in his death. By it we share in his resurrection. Through it we are reborn by the Holy Spirit."[6]

God calls us to step into the swirling waters, to wade into the deep, to drown our small ideas, let go of certain dreams or sins, to submerge our narrowed hopes to hear again the call of Christ. We emerge, dripping like

Jesus, to face a new future. We are a baptismal people, a river people, who now come to the Jordan in our daily experience. Baptism reminds us that we can encounter God's grace as a flooding, a drenching, an inundation and a drowning.

The spiritual journey is a passage into greater degrees of spiritual freedom and release from captivity, so that we might be totally available to God: freedom is *from* something, to open up new possibilities *for* something. It is a significant theme in the *Spiritual Exercises* of Ignatius Loyola—Christ cutting us free from all kinds of attachments that tie us down, such as false securities, dependencies, and addictions. In his "Fundamental Principle" Ignatius encourages a radical *indifference*, by which he means "detachment":

> Man has been created to praise, reverence and serve our Lord God, thereby saving his soul. . . . Therefore we need to train ourselves to be impartial in our attitude towards all created reality . . . we do not set our hearts on good health as against bad health, prosperity as against poverty, a good reputation as against a bad one. . . . The one thing we desire, the one thing we choose is what is more likely to achieve the purpose of our creating.[7]

Passing through Storms and Chaos

The waters can denote and represent those traumatic periods we face in the spiritual journey. The psalms pierce the skies with cries to God amidst trouble:

> He reached down from on high, he took me;
>   he drew me out of mighty waters. (Ps 18:16)

> Save me, O God,
>   for the waters have come up to my neck.
> I have come into deep waters,
>   and the flood sweeps over me. (Ps 69:1-2)

> The flood would have swept us away,
>   the torrent would have gone over us;
>   then over us would have gone the raging waters. (Ps 124:4-5)

> Let everyone cry out to you at a time of distress,
>   the rush of mighty waters shall not reach me.
> You are a hiding-place for me;
>   you preserve me from trouble. (Ps 32:6-7)

> God is our refuge and strength,
>> a very present help in trouble.
> We will not fear,
>> though the mountains shake in the heart of the sea;
>> though its waters roar and foam,
>> though the mountains tremble with its tumult. (Ps. 46)

And in the prophets God gives this reassurance: "When you pass through the waters, I will be with you" (Isa 43.2).

In the worldview of the ancient Near East, which forms the background to the biblical accounts, the sea was feared as the abode of chaos. The waters were brimming with demons and monsters. We even know their names—here lurk Leviathan and Rahab (Ps 74:13-14). The very mention of the sea evokes the primordial chaos of Genesis 1, where "darkness covered the face of the deep, while a wind from God swept over the waters." The stories of the storm on the lake—found in Mark 4; 6; Matthew 8; and Luke 8—evoke this background, as Jesus shouts to the demon of the deep, "Be muzzled!" (Mark 4:39, my translation). The image of a fragile and vulnerable boat on stormy, turbulent waters resonates powerfully with our spiritual experience of feeling alone, abandoned, or facing what seem to be insuperable problems.

Voyaging into the Deep

The biggest question for pilgrims is this: "Dare I move out of my comfort zone, represented by feet firmly planted on *terra firma*, and venture forth to do things differently?" This challenge resonates with the challenge Jesus gave to Peter at the Sea of Galilee: "Put out into the deep!" (Luke 5:4). The image of the sea invites us to leave behind the security of being on familiar land and move out into unchartered waters. The shoreline represents the brink of new possibilities. It represents the limit of our own confidence, the edge of our sense of security. But this is a threshold we must cross if we are to live as pilgrims in this world, people on the move, people going places with God.

The image of the sea invites us to confront our fears and anxieties about the future, represented in the uncertain waves. We are crippled into inaction by fear, and in our personal life we may hang back from a new venture or new expression of ministry by the fear of failure. The sea can represent the fear of the unknown, aspects of mission that for us are yet unfamiliar waters.

We recall the Israelites hovering on the brink of the Red Sea in the exodus event. They were faced with the impossibility of crossing the angry and formidable waters and the risk of being trapped by the pursuing forces of the pharaoh. To his surprise, the key to salvation was in Moses' own hand, and it was with his action of striking the waters that the miracle of the splitting of the sea occurred. In Jewish spirituality, the "splitting of the seas" has become a powerful symbol of facing the impossible with God: God makes the impossible possible, but needs men and women to be prepared to plunge into a risky synergy with the divine.

Overcoming Barriers

In the journey of prayer we sometimes sense that something is holding us back from advancing: in the spiritual pathway there are hazards, dangers, barriers, and roadblocks. It is healthy to be able to identify and name possible resistances within ourselves—this is the first step toward an overcoming and breakthrough.[8]

We can be held back by a sense of boredom in the spiritual life. A repeated tendency to ignore certain gospel truths that claim attention also delays our progress. A habitual repetition of patterns of prayer might actually be a strategy for avoiding the deeper and more risky encounter with God: the prayer book becomes the roadblock! Sometimes doubts, fears, or a sense of worthlessness or shame might pull us in a backward direction. Obsessions, attachments or addictions might cause us to get fixated or stuck. False views of self or distorted views of God, perhaps juvenile or childish in origin, do not help us move ahead. Self-knowledge is a wonderful grace enabling us to bring these sort of things to a spiritual director. Sometimes, of course, we will not be conscious or aware of our blindspots and prejudices and need others to lovingly tell us. Resistances to God's grace can turn out to be positive, because they are a sign that something is happening!

Psalm 18:30 invites us to dismantle walls: "With You I will break down barricades; with the help of my God I will scale any wall." An urgent task in the spiritual life is to examine our *own* walls and lower the self-protective barriers that we unconsciously erect to protect ourselves from getting too close to what might challenge us. We need the grace to first recognize and then chip away at our own walls and defenses. This is a basic requirement for pilgrims—to be ready for some measure of brokenness and honesty, as we expose our hearts and minds to new insights and new ways of seeing things.

Our Need for Maps

In our personal lives and times of prayer we often find ourselves thirsting for something more. We need to recognize the signs and clues that are indicating to us that it is time to move on. The signs that we are ready to embark on a spiritual adventure might begin with a sense of holy listlessness or restlessness, a certain discontent with our present spiritual life, a holy dissatisfaction, and a dawning sense that God is calling us forward.

Travelers find helpful a map or guide to clarify the journey. The church fathers began to recognize a pattern in people's spiritual lives that crystallized as a "Triple Way." The journey begins with a radical turning toward God in repentance, opening ourselves to the cleansing grace of Christ (*via purgativa*). Pilgrims next learn the truths of the faith and clarify moral goals (*via illuminativa*). The ultimate aim is complete sanctification by the Spirit who unites every Christian with God (*via unitiva*).[9] Leech draws attention to its scriptural roots: "The traditional 'Three Ways' (purgation, illumination, union) are not alien mystical forms imposed artificially on the gospel, but they arise out of the very features of the gospel message— repentance, life in the Spirit, and perfection. The motion of spiritual progress is an essential element in the biblical revelation."[10] Thornton comments: "The Three Ways remain fundamental to Christian spirituality, and essential in spiritual guidance, but as a map or chart of the spiritual country, as a "back-cloth," not as a rigid program."[11] How did this begin?

Origen (ca. 185–254) was the first writer to conceive of the soul's pilgrimage in terms of a threefold path, which is worked out within the encounter of the Christian tradition with Platonic philosophy. In his *Commentary on the Song of Songs* Origen affirms:

> And so the rational being, growing at each successive stage, not as it grew when in this life in the flesh or body and in the soul, but increasing in mind and intelligence, advances as a mind already perfect to perfect knowledge, no longer hindered by its former carnal senses, but developing in intellectual power, ever approaching the pure and gazing "face to face," if I may so speak, on the causes of things.[12]

He sees in the three Wisdom books ascribed to Solomon an emerging threefold pattern: Proverbs provides a moral orientation; Ecclesiastes discerns what is profitable in creation; and the Song of Songs celebrates the path to union with God. Origen sees in this pattern a progress of successive stages by which the soul is invited to advance toward God. Here lies the genesis of the Triple Way, profoundly shaped by Origen's Christian—

platonic anthropology: the goal in view is for the soul (*psyche*) to become free from the attentions of the body in order to contemplate God as *nous*, mind. This is a mysticism in which there is a creative but unresolved tension between inherited Platonic concepts and the still-emerging Christian doctrine of the incarnation of the Word.

Evagrius (ca. 346–99) develops a threefold pattern for the soul in somewhat differing terminology. First he identifies *praktike*: the practice and development of the virtues and overcoming vices. Along these lines, *ascesis* involves struggle with temptations, the passions, and the demonic. A second stage, termed *physike*, is marked by contemplation of how the world exists in God's *logos*. Now the soul can see more clearly than before the spiritual dynamics at work—that is, recognizing and discerning good and evil, angels and demons. Greater detachment enables greater attentiveness to God, a movement from the material to the immaterial. A sign that the soul has achieved this stage is its readiness to help others on the spiritual path.

In the third stage, *theologia*, the soul is capable of a contemplation that is beyond words or images. The soul reaches its true vocation as *nous*, or mind, attuned to God. The soul achieves a *gnosis* (knowledge) that entails the stripping away of all definite thoughts. Louth calls Evagrius an intellectualist: "the goal of the mystical life is conceived of as the supreme activity of the mind or intellect."[13]

Theologia involves *gnosis*: "If you are a theologian, you pray in truth; if you pray in truth, you are a theologian." Evagrius marks an important point in the evolving story of the Triple Way. Already he reveals how such a map for the spiritual journey can inspire progress. Louis Bouyer notes with caution, however, how Evagrius makes an overly rigid distinction between *theologia* and the contemplation of God in himself, and the purifications preceding it. As Bouyer has written: "Following him, there has been too great a tendency to detach the mystical experience, as it came to be called, from the whole ascetical and doctrinal substructure presupposed by it, reducing it finally to an extraordinary experience, distinguishable and perhaps even definable by certain mainly negative psychological criteria."[14] It is best not to see this in terms of a linear progression, whereby one must follow successive stages, but rather as three themes that recur again and again and deepen in intensity. Modern approaches to spiritual development are alert to the cyclical nature of the journey.[15]

Navigation: Facing Different Directions

The language of pilgrims, then, encompasses geographic metaphors that can help orientate ourselves on the journey. In the Orthodox eucharistic liturgy the deacon cries out repeatedly "Look to the East!" We are called to be ready for the *parousia*, and live in expectation and hope. In the East the sun arises, of course; it is the place of the new dawn. In Luke 24 the two disciples are walking in the wrong direction, as they follow a road that leads away from the holy city of passion and resurrection, and the risen Christ will walk with them. John Donne develops this theme in his poem "Riding Westward." On Good Friday 1613 he became aware, on horseback,

> that I am carried towards the west
> This day, when my soul's form bends towards the east.

He rode into the place where "Sin had benighted all." But he was ready to change and in the last line of the poem resolves: "I'll turn my face."

Spiritual directors may be imagined as navigators of the soul who can read the unfolding signs and clues within the experience of the person they accompany, or as map-readers who can spot the traditional reference points. Paul lists as one of the gifts of the Spirit *kubernetes*—often translated "administration," but better as "navigation" or "helmsmanship." For Paul, the art of discerning the Spirit's movement, the art of recognizing the need of the moment, is akin to the skill of the ship's pilot and steersman who, working collaboratively alongside the captain, coxswain, and the entire crew, will guide the ship in its adventures. In the seventh century John Climacus of Sinai wrote of the need for courageous spiritual directors using this image: "A ship with a good navigator comes safely to port, God willing." [16] In the Syriac tradition, Christ is depicted as a mariner guiding his people. [17] The ancient liturgy of the Ethiopian Church calls on God as a pilot: "Pilot of the soul, Guide of the righteous, and Glory of the Saints. Grant us, O Lord, eyes of knowledge ever to see Thee, and ears also to hearken to thy Word alone." [18]

Questions for Reflection and Discussion

1. What is your experience of encountering the unexpected on your spiritual journey? Did this lead you to conversion or to change?

2. In the book of Isaiah God says: "remove every obstruction from my people's way" (57:14) and "build up the highway, clear it of stones" (62:10). What impediments to your spiritual progress can

you name? What roadblocks do you need to overcome if you are to advance in the spiritual journey?

3. Can you identify any ways in which you are becoming sidetracked or tempted to go off on a tangent from your spiritual path?

4. One of the most attractive images of spiritual directors is that of companions—as fellow travelers or accompaniers walking along the road. What is your experience of walking with another along the spiritual pathway? When was such accompaniment most helpful to you?

Further Reading

Mulholland, M. Robert. *Invitation to a Journey: A Road Map for Spiritual Formation.* Downers Grove, IL: InterVarsityPress, 1993.

Riddell, Mike. *Godzone: A Guide to the Travels of the Soul.* Oxford: Lion, 1992.

Silf, Margaret. *Wayfaring: A Gospel Journey into Life.* London: Darton, Longman & Todd, 2001.

6

The Adventurous Language
of Explorers and Seekers

Forgetting what lies behind,
and straining forward to what lies
ahead, I press on toward the goal,
for the prize of the heavenly call of
God in Christ Jesus.

—Phil 3:13-14

Within the contours of the spiritual landscape we encounter features powerfully representing key aspects of the prayer journey. Here we traverse the desert, ascend the mountain, cross the bridge, and descend to the cave. We are invited to become fearless adventurers, courageous explorers of the spiritual terrain. This imagery beckons us forward into risky places along our spiritual odyssey and quest, summoning us to curiosity and fresh discoveries.

Encountering the Desert

When Christians speak of a "desert experience" or a "wilderness time," they often refer to a bleakness, a time of testing, a sense of desolation. When we recall Jesus' forty days in the Judean desert, we generally focus on his temptations, his grappling with shortcuts to success held out tantalizingly before him. But the desert—indeed, like "the dark night of the soul"—turns out to be a creative place of growth and breakthrough. The desert suggests for us much more than trial and stress. It is, as Mark 1:13 tells us, not only a place of wild beasts, but also a place of angels! Let us recall that for Moses and the children of Israel, the Sinai desert was not only a place of fear and danger. Precisely the same place, in fact, was also the locus of theophany and revelation! In the desert the nomadic

Israelites came to realize new things about themselves. It was a place of radical discovery. They came to a fresh understanding of their dignity and calling as God's people (Exod 19:1-8). They encountered God in fresh ways, not only sensing his presence among them, as represented by the Tabernacle that moved with them, but also the awesome gift of the Torah to Moses atop Mount Sinai. As they were offered a covenant, they started to realize some of the possibilities and opportunities God had in store for them. So the desert experience was far from grim. God made himself known.

So, too, Jesus found his desert sojourn to be highly formative. He went into the desert with those words ringing in his ears: "You are my beloved Son, with you I am well pleased!" The forty days gave him the opportunity to relish this affirmation and come to terms with his vocation and identity. Amidst the rocks, he clarified his mission. The Gospel of Mark tells us that he emerged from the desert announcing these words: "The time is fulfilled, and the kingdom of God has come near" (Mark 1:15). So we can conclude that in the desert Jesus came to a clear vision of his mission and a crisp understanding of his message: the reign of God. In the heat of the desert, irrelevant ideas melted away. He came to see what was crucial—and what was not.

As we reflect on the desert as a source of metaphors for the spiritual life, then, we see that it can be suggestive of discovery, growth, and insight. It is not all doom and gloom! God is at work amidst the rocks and canyons. The physical desert, so vital to Jesus and the early church, opens up for us a challenging range of metaphors.

The Empty Desert of the Soul

In Christian spirituality the physical wildernesses of the desert fathers and mothers became symbolic of the soul—its thirst and longing for the Spirit, in particular. Once again, the outer landscape speaks of the *inscape*: physicality points to spirituality, and outer realities to the inner. The desert speaks powerfully of our spiritual poverty. It confronts us with the aridity of our lives and alerts us to recognize where there might be signs of emptiness. As Macarius wrote: "We have an insatiable longing for the Spirit, to shine out—the more spiritual gifts we enjoy, the more insatiable is the heavenly desire in our hearts, the more hungry and thirsty we are for more grace."[1] Thus the desert of prayer becomes a place of deep renewal and experience of the Holy Spirit. Isaiah the prophet sees the barrenness and emptiness of the desert as a symbol of humanity's need—a natural analogy for our need of God. The desert dramatically represents spiritual poverty and human thirst for the divine, and God promises: "I will pour water on the thirsty land, and streams on the dry ground. I will pour my Spirit upon your descendents." (Isa 44:3; see also 35:1-10 and 41:17-20). Dare you thirst for more of God in prayer?

The Open Desert of the Soul

The physical desert is a place of exposure to sun and wind where there is no hiding place. So in prayer we become naked before God, exposing heart and mind to the wind of his Spirit and the warmth of his love. The desert is a place of persistent erosion, where wind and even water wear down the resistance of stubborn rocks and refashion their shapes. There are unremitting processes of disintegration at work in the desert landscape, as well as processes of formation and building up. This speaks of the vulnerability necessary in the God-seeking soul. In prayer we become susceptible to God and open to his ever-creative remolding. In prayer, our normal guards melt away so that God is permitted to reshape our life and our priorities. As in the desert all props are gone and only essential things matter, so prayer demands utter honesty, permits no masks. Before God we face up in utter honesty to the realities of our lives. Dare you open up a space for God in your life?

The Lonely Desert of the Soul

The desert calls us to solitude, to letting go of the clamor of things, so that loneliness may turn to *aloneness.* Jesus not only prefaced his ministry with his desert-time, but he also punctuated his ministry by regular retreat into the hills. When in Jerusalem, he withdrew to the Garden of Gethsemane, nestling at the foot of the Mount of Olives outside the noise and demands of the city. Such places are designated in the Greek text as an *eremos*—a lonely place, a place set apart. Jesus used these times for attuning with keener focus to the Father's voice, for discerning priorities. The desert calls us most of all, to listening, to God, to our own hearts. Dare you get alone with God, and with yourself?

So when we talk of the "desert time" or "going through a wilderness," we may testify to the experience of fresh discoveries of God—and of ourselves!

Scaling the Heights

Many spiritual writers, especially male authors, explore prayer as an ascent to God.[2] In the Scriptures, the mountaintop is the place of theophany and revelation: we think of mysterious Mount Sinai, snow-capped Mount Hermon, and the awesome Mount Tabor, where the transfiguration took place. Writers see prayer as accompanying Jesus into the upper reaches of prayer. The ascent of the mountain will take stamina, resolution, and determination. There will be plenty of distractions and temptations to take shortcuts. What is needed is singleness of heart to go with Jesus, wherever he leads.

In addition to the mountains of the Bible, passages like Jacob's ladder stretching up toward heaven with angels ascending and descending (Gen 28:12; John 1:51) inspire thoughts of reaching up to God. In the history of Christian spirituality the metaphor of ascent prevails. The way to God seems to be up, up, up. Writing at the monastery at the foot of Mount Sinai, the abbot John Climacus (579–649) suggests that the virtues form thirty rungs on the *Ladder of Divine Ascent.* Saint Bonaventure writes of the "mind's ascent to God" in his work *The Journey of the Mind into God.* Even St. John of the Cross, in his masterpiece *The Ascent of Mount Carmel,* uses this model of going up to God and leaving worldly things behind. The fourteenth-century English mystic Walter Hilton viewed the Christian life in terms of *The Scale (or Ladder) of Ascent.* A recurring theme in these works is the necessity for detachment—withdrawal from daily demands in order to enter prayer, conceived as a sacred space, as a different world.[3] Meanwhile, St. Benedict speaks of the ladder of humility: "We may call our body and soul the sides of this ladder, into which our divine vocation has fitted the various steps of humility and discipline as we ascend."[4]

The letter to the Hebrews celebrates Moses as a pilgrim and wayfarer (11:23-29). Influenced by Platonic ideas in the fourth century, Gregory of Nyssa uses the climbing of mountains as a model of Christian perfection in his *Life of Moses.* Gregory sees Moses as representing the Christian who is continually urged by God to keep moving forward. In his *Life of Moses,* he traces a map of the Christian pilgrimage as it is suggested to him by the Exodus accounts.[5] It begins with baptism, prefigured in the crossing of the Red Sea, liberating a person from the captivity not of Pharaoh but of sin. The Christian pilgrim's journey, like the trek through the wilderness, will be marked by God's provision (e.g., manna and water from the rock), God's guidance (the pillar of cloud), human failure, and spiritual battles (as represented in the conflict with Amalekites). Ultimately this leads to the ascent of the mountain of divine knowledge, represented in Sinai.

Gregory notices that when Moses climbs a mountain he does not relax in his success but rather finds himself in a position to glimpse the further horizons and greater peaks to which God is beckoning him. From the crest, he can view the other mountains he is impelled to climb. So Gregory develops a dynamic view of spiritual development, character-ized by *epekstasis*: a vision of the Christian life as continually evolving and progressing, energized by the Holy Spirit. For Gregory, the disciple should never stand still, but continually stretch himself or herself toward the "upward call" and so reach one's full potential in Christ.[6] Each stage reached in the spiritual journey is but a beginning, not an end. The ex-plorer can never say: "I have arrived!" In Gregory's eyes, the greatest sin is that of complacency, of resting on one's laurels. Gregory's vision is one of lifelong learning or rather, eternal progress.

Negatively, the metaphor of ascent resonates with the modern desire for self-advancement, the seeking of promotion, "going up the ladder," and acquiring ever greater power and status. It suggests that one must renounce the world and get away from it in order to find God. But we may notice the helpful aspects of this imagery: the need for determination and focus in the spiritual journey. We experience both exhaustion and exhilaration—periods when prayer seems an uphill struggle and rarer times when we feel as if we stand on the mountaintop, breathing a different air! Those called to accompany others in their prayer journey might be inspired by picturing the Sherpa guides from Tibet and Nepal, famous for the remark-able assistance they provide to Himalayan mountaineering expeditions, including the ascent of Mount Everest. These mountain guides are hardy, experienced, and skilled. They know the joys and dangers of the ascent and descent. They have trod this way many times before, and they have come to an understanding of the terrain, its beauty, and its risks. They know where there are hazardous and slippery paths. They watch out for the signs of altitude sickness in the climbers. They walk beside the explorer and help to carry the load and share the burden. Sherpas are keenly aware that they tread on sacred ground: the mountain is a holy place, not to be "conquered," but to be approached with awe and respect. Theirs is a costly ministry, for they are not immune to the dangers of the mount or to the risk of slipping. This vivid image of spiritual accompaniment resonates with the spiritual journey depicted as *ascesis* or training (compare Paul's picture of the spiritual athlete in 1 Cor 9:24-27).

In the nineteenth century, Térèse of Lisieux spoke of her need for an *ascenseur*—a lift or elevator—and she saw the little way of spiritual childhood as a way that lifts one up to God: "I wish to find the way to go to Heaven by a very straight, short, completely new little way. We are in a century of inventions: now one does not even have to take the trouble to climb the steps of a stairway; in the homes of the rich an elevator replaces them nicely. I, too, would like to find an elevator to lift me up to Jesus, for I am too little to climb the rough stairway of perfection."[7] Interestingly, Térèse suffered from vertigo and dizziness regularly, but she was still attracted by the image of ascent!

Crossing the Bridge

In *The Dialogue* Catherine of Siena (1347–80) develops her vision of a progressive spiritual journey through the imagery of Christ the Bridge, which stretches above a treacherous chasm.[8] Munro explains:

> Climbing and reclimbing the stairs provide continuous opportunity to grow more perfect. The bridge between heaven and earth is available to everyone desirous of eternal life. Christ's teaching as well as his body is the way promised in the scripture. The bridge terminates in the gate to heaven. Christ is lifted up from the earth as a bridge lifts off one side of a chasm to reach the other. Sin had created a chasm: a road that was there before was now entirely broken up and impassible, in its place a raging torrent that no one can cross without drowning. The bridge is the crucified Christ, arching over the chasm in stairs on which we rise through love—our love, but really his love. . . . This bridge is paved with the stones of Christ's virtue, cemented with the "living lime" of God's love, the very Godhead, and with his blood. . . . Christ is himself the living stone upon which we must be added to the structure with the same mortar of living lime and blood. . . . The bridge symbolizes Christ as necessary mediator of grace through whom alone perfection can be achieved. It also symbolizes the journey from sinfulness to holiness.[9]

Plumbing the Depths

Cosby writes of the descending God: "If God is going down and we are going up, it is obvious that we are going in different directions. . . . We will be evading God and missing the whole purpose of our existence."[10] Paul Tillich spoke of God as "the ground of being," and in his work *The Shaking of the Foundations* he invites us to rediscover the metaphor of the depths of God: "Most of our life continues on the surface. We are enslaved by the routine of our daily lives. . . . We are in constant motion and never stop to plunge into the depth. We talk and talk and never listen to the voices speaking to our depth and from our depth. . . . It is comfortable to live on the surface. . . . It is painful to break away from it and to descend into an unknown ground."[11]

In this imagery we are summoned to quit superficial living and risk a descent into the depths, where we may find God, and in the process, rediscover ourselves. As spiritual writer Richard Foster put it: "Superficiality is the curse of our age. . . . The desperate need today is not for a greater number of intelligent people, or gifted people, but for deep people."[12] The image of the "the cave of the heart" derives from Hindu spirituality, but it resonates strongly with the Christian tradition. Elijah encounters God at the mouth of the cave on Mount Horeb—the cave in the mountain (1 Kgs 17). The psalms cry to God from the depths: "I am counted among those who go down to the Pit" (Ps 88:4).

With the descent of the Word into the depths of the earth, the cave becomes a symbol of salvation. The Orthodox liturgy notices the significance of the cave of Bethlehem, celebrating the paradox of the Maker of the heavens coming to be contained in the earth: "Triumph O Zion . . . receive the Creator who is contained with a cave!"[13] A compline hymn wonders at the divine condescension: "When the creation beheld Thee born in a cave, who hast hung the whole earth in the void above the waters, it was seized with amazement and cried: 'There is none holy save Thee, O Lord.'"[14] Christ is entombed in a cave and it is from the depths that he rises to new life. So the cave represents the mysterious workings of God, his hidden purposes, often unfathomable and unsearchable: "we speak God's wisdom, secret and hidden . . . the Spirit searches everything, even the depths of God" (1 Cor 2:7, 11). The darkness of the cave speaks to us of the mystery of God: "Can you find out the deep things of God? Can you find out the limit of the Almighty? . . . Deeper than Sheol—what can you know?" (Job 11:7) With Paul we say: "O the depth of the riches and wisdom and knowledge of God! How unsearchable are his judgments and how inscrutable his ways!" (Rom 11:33).[15] We join the psalmist in his prayer: "You desire truth in the inward being; therefore teach me wisdom in my secret heart" (51:6).

Questions for Reflection and Discussion

1. How does the language of explorers reverberate in your own soul?

2. Recall a phase in your spiritual journey that felt like passing through a desert. What positive aspects there can you now name? How would you describe the experience of radical exposure to God?

3. Which image are you more drawn to: climbing the mountain or plumbing the depths? Can you say why?

4. Which aspects of the spiritual landscape are you discovering now? What new discoveries have you made in the last year?

5. How helpful do you find the language of being "an explorer of the interior space"? What does it suggest to you about the terrain of the spiritual life?

Further Reading

Adams, Ian. *Cave, Refectory, Road: Monastic Rhythms for Daily Living.* Collegeville, MN: Liturgical Press, 2012.

Miles, Margaret. *The Image and Practice of Holiness: A Critique of the Classic Manuals of Devotion.* London: SCM, 1989.

Ramon, Brother. *The Prayer Mountain: Exploring the High Places of Prayer.* Norwich: Canterbury Press, 1998.

Silf, Margaret. *Landscapes of Prayer: Finding God in Your World and Your Life.* London: Lion Hudson, 2011.

Ward, Benedicta, trans. *The Sayings of the Desert Fathers: The Alphabetical Collection.* Revised edition. Collegeville, MN: Liturgical Press, 1984.

7

The Creative Language
of Builders and Citizens

Prompted to see my bliss above
    the skies,
How often did I lift mine eyes
Beyond the spheres!
Dame Nature told me that there
    was endless space
Within my soul

— Thomas Traherne, "Felicity" [1]

We do not need to look to the heavens for spiritual imagery; it is close at hand. Here we explore the inner spaces expressed in spatial, urban, domestic, and architectural metaphors. Complementing the dynamic imagery of journey and pilgrimage, the biblical and Christian tradition beckons us to metaphors celebrating the divine seeking residence in human lives. Come and explore the building and the city, the temple, house, castle, and prison.

The Temple, Old and New

The word "contemplation" derives from *con* and *templum*—meaning, literally, *together with the sacred space.* In contemplation we enter the sanctuary of the soul, the temple of the spirit and discover God within. The theme of God's own dwelling place runs throughout the Scriptures. With the building of the first temple, and the placing of the ark of the covenant within the holy of holies, the psalms celebrate God's residence set in the midst of the people: "How lovely is your dwelling place, O Lord of hosts!" (Ps 84:1). With the coming of Jesus, God establishes his tabernacle in a new place: "And the Word became flesh and lived among us" (John 1:14). In the perspective of the gospels, Jesus is the new temple itself (John 2:13-22). Ephesians takes the imagery further: "In him [Christ Jesus] the whole structure is joined together and grows into a holy temple in the Lord; in whom you also are built together spiritually into a dwelling-place for God" (2:19-22).

Jesus himself delights in building-metaphors as he inaugurates the construction of the kingdom. God was calling him to form something new, beautiful, and indestructible, his *ecclesia*: "And I tell you, you are Peter, and on this rock I will build my church, and the gates of Hades will not prevail against it" (Matt 16:18). He declares: "Everyone then who hears these words of mine and acts on them will be like a wise man who built his house on rock" (Matt 7:24). Jesus makes plain the cost of discipleship: "For which of you, intending to build a tower, does not first sit down and estimate the cost. . . . Otherwise . . . all who see it will begin to ridicule him, saying, 'This fellow began to build and was not able to finish'" (Luke 14:28-29).

Christian formation attests to God's ever-creative process of shaping our lives, God's awesome creativity. Jeremiah's image of the potter working on the clay (18:1-6) reminds us that God not only makes us of dust of the earth, he wants to shape us. God can do wonderful things with the "raw material" of a human life yielded to his hands. Formation is a process by which a person gets reshaped. New Testament writers explore the pastoral dimensions of the powerful building and formation metaphor. Paul calls himself a builder: "According to the grace of God given to me, like a skilled master builder I laid a foundation, and someone else is building on it. Each builder must choose with care how to build on it. . . . Do you not know that you are God's temple and that God's Spirit dwells in you?" (1 Cor 3:10, 17). What skills do you think Paul utilized in building Christian community, and what building skills do you seek to develop in your ministry? What materials and resources are available for strengthening spirituality in your community?

Peter calls us to be reshaped: "Come to him, a living stone, though rejected by mortals yet chosen and precious in God's sight, and like living stones, let yourselves be built into a spiritual house" (1 Pet 2:4-9). Stones need to be "dressed" or reshaped with chisel and hammer before they can be used—this is essential so that they fit together properly in the structure under construction. In what ways have you experienced your Christian formation among "living stones" as a painful process? In what ways do you expect your ministry to be a costly business?

The Interior Castle

Teresa of Ávila (1515–82) employs vivid images to describe the changes that can take place in prayer. Depicting the soul as a crystal castle with many rooms and with Christ dwelling at the center, she invites the reader to trace a journey through successive stages in order to reach a state of mystical union:

> I began to think of the soul as if it were a castle made of a single diamond or of very clear crystal, in which there are many rooms, just as in Heaven there are many mansions. Now if we think carefully over this, the soul of the righteous one is nothing but a paradise, in which, as God tells us, He takes His delight. For what do you think a room will be like which is the delight of a King so mighty, so wise, so pure and so full of all that is good? I can find nothing with which to compare the great beauty of a soul and its great capacity . . . (though) the very fact that His majesty says it is made in His image means that we can hardly form any conception of the soul's great dignity and beauty. . . .
>
> Let us imagine that this castle contains many mansions, some above, others below, others at each side; and in the centre and midst of them all is the chiefest mansion where the most secret things pass between God and the soul.[2]

The image conveys the beauty and potential of the soul; the door to the castle, and indeed its weaving corridor, is the experience of prayer. Rowan Williams observes:

> If the soul is a home for God, it is a home with an enormous abundance of rooms, and we shall need to know where we are if we are not to be deceived and think we have encountered God when we have not . . . the journey inward is a journey to the place where God's love meets and mingles with the life of the soul, and thus we need to keep moving through the rooms until we find the middle of what sounds remarkably like a maze. . . . We do not know where the boundaries are if we never move forward and walk into them. . . . We need to know what we are capable of, positively and negatively.[3]

The first three rooms of Teresa's interior castle represent an increasing detachment from the things of the world and a process of deepening repentance and humility. In the first room of self-knowledge, Teresa cries: "O souls redeemed by the blood of Jesus Christ! Learn to understand yourselves! . . . The soul's capacity is much greater than we can realize."[4] In the second room we are called to conquer the pull to turn back to the attractions of the world, in order to remain very focused and single-minded in the interior journey. The third room describes the stability and predictability of respectable routines and normal disciplines of the Christian life, like active discursive meditation. A sign or indicator that the soul is ready to move on from these reveals itself in a holy restlessness or discontent with unfulfilling dutiful praying—a craving for a greater interior freedom and a desire to jump off the treadmill of Christian life.

A significant turning point in the journey comes with entry into the fourth room, a place of new discovery that opens us up to "supernatural" prayer: "Supernatural prayer is where God takes over. It is also called infused contemplation, passive prayer, mystical prayer, or infused prayer. All labels, again, mean the same thing. This type of prayer means that God is communicating with the person."[5] Teresa advises: "The important thing is not to think much, but to love much."[6] A letting-go of former restrictive practices of prayer enables a movement from the primacy of ego to the initiative of God.

But there is no need to rest even here: go deeper into God through Teresa's remaining rooms: the fifth mansion is a place of liberation where the soul breaks free from its chrysalis or cocoon and learns to "fly" in a new freedom. In the sixth mansion the pilgrim-soul stumbles on a glittering treasury in the inner reaches of the castle: a range of spiritual gifts. Here Teresa speaks of the soul's betrothal to God, while in the seventh she uses the daring language of mystical marriage to describe union with God as an abiding awareness and permanent consciousness of unity with the indwelling Christ. As Teresa provides a sketch of the spiritual life through the imagery of one room leading to another in a mysterious castle of prayer, the main point is: whatever room of prayer you find yourself in, this room has a door facing you right now, beckoning you to yet-unexplored reaches of prayer. Don't get stuck in one room. Go on, try the next door, see where it leads!

Crossing Thresholds and Opening Doors

John of the Cross also used the image of the soul as a house in his *Ascent of Mount Carmel:* "My house being now all stilled." The opening of doors is an associated biblical image. The risen Lord calls out to us: "Listen! I am standing at the door, knocking; if you hear my voice and open the door, I will come in to you and eat with you, and you with me" (Rev 3:20). In his narrative of the early church, Luke describes the pushing back of doors: "When they arrived, they called the church together and related all that God had done with them, and how he had opened a door of faith for the

Gentiles" (Acts 14:27). Paul too develops the domestic metaphor of the open door: "A wide door for effective work has opened to me, and there are many adversaries" (1 Cor 16:19). He relates: "When I came to Troas to proclaim the good news of Christ, a door was opened for me in the Lord" (2 Cor 2:12). He asks: "At the same time pray for us as well that God will open to us a door for the word, that we may declare the mystery of Christ, for which I am in prison" (Col 4:3).

Spiritual Imprisonment

When Paul writes about spiritual captivity and liberation he is developing this imagery from his firsthand experience of incarceration. Three times in the book of Acts the apostles are set free from physical jails and from actual chains (Acts 5; 12; 16), and on each occasion Luke describes the process of gaining liberation very graphically. In Jerusalem after the apostles were arrested and thrown into prison, an angel opens the prison door (5:18). In Philippi, the jailer "put them [Paul and Silas] in the innermost cell and fastened their feet in the stocks" (16:24). Luke gives us a vivid account of the liberating earthquake in which "all the doors were opened and everyone's chains were unfastened" (16:26). This inspired Charles Wesley's hymn celebrating his own inner liberation:

> Long my imprisoned spirit lay,
> Fast bound in sin and nature's night;
> Thine eye diffused a quick'ning ray—
> I woke, the dungeon flamed with light;
> My chains fell off, my heart was free;
> I rose, went forth and followed Thee.[7]

From his incarceration in either Ephesus or Rome, Paul writes to the Philippians a letter that celebrates freedom in Christ as its main theme. Paul is clear that Gentiles do not need to worry about constricting requirements in the Jewish law like circumcision. Later Paul writes: "There is therefore now no condemnation for those who are in Christ Jesus. For the law of the Spirit of life in Christ Jesus has set you free from the law of sin and of death" (Rom 8:1, 2). Indeed his vision for the freedom God gives becomes wider still: he expresses the cosmic longing that "the creation itself will be set free from its bondage to decay and will obtain the freedom of the glory of the children of God" (Rom 8:21). He celebrates the liberty that the Holy Spirit enables: "Now the Lord is the Spirit, and where the Spirit of the Lord is, there is freedom" (2 Cor 3:17).

In the gospels, Jesus promises: "If the Son makes you free, you will be free indeed" (John 8:36). The theme of imprisonment gives us a rich vocabulary with which to name those inner attitudes and attitudes of heart that have become enslaving, and helps us to identify those bondages in our thinking creating crippling mindsets. Jesus the liberator comes to set us free from narrow and negative thinking. He comes to release us from false images of God and false images of humanity and human potential. He comes to unbind us from the bondages of guilt and shame, and from the distortions wrought in our attitudes by the ego. He unbinds us from false attachments.

We see this very vividly in the life of St. Francis of Assisi, called by liberation theologian Leonardo Boff a "model of human liberation."[8] Thomas of Celano in his biography gives us several dimensions of the freedom into which Christ led Francis, which alerts us to the types of liberation we ourselves can experience. His *Life of St Francis* (1229) declares: "Those who experienced the greatness of his soul know how well how free and freeing (*liber et liberalis*) he was in everything, how intrepid and fearless in all circumstances."[9]

Francis is both liberated and liberator. He is freed from ambition, from avarice and from anxiety about possessions. His father physically incarcerates him but he finds a release, outer and inner. Embracing the despised leper he finds himself set free from prejudice. By the experience of forgiveness he is released from the attachments of the past. He becomes available to God for a radical ministry of reconciliation. In our own spiritual life, we need first to give name to the captivities and things that hold us down, in order to enter into the liberation Christ can bring.

The City of God

In the Scriptures one detects a certain ambiguity toward the city and its symbolism. Early in the Old Testament, the city of Babel becomes a symbol of pride and stubbornness as well as a place of human achievement: "Then they said, 'Come, let us build ourselves a city, and a tower with its top in the heavens, and let us make a name for ourselves; otherwise we shall be scattered abroad upon the face of the whole earth'" (Gen 11:4). Yet at the heart of the Old Testament narrative, the city on Zion becomes God's chosen dwelling place as the temple is built.

Jesus reveals an ambivalence to the city of Jerusalem: it becomes for him the place both of passion and resurrection. He hails it as "the city of the great King" (Matt 5:35) but weeping over it (Luke 19: 41), he laments: "Jerusalem, Jerusalem, the city that kills the prophets and stones those who are sent to it!" (Matt 23:37). The city which witnesses the crucifixion and rejection of his mission is destined to be the very locus of the Spirit's empowerment, and so he commands his disciples: "I am sending upon you what my Father promised; so stay here in the city until you have been clothed with power from on high" (Luke 24:49). For Jesus, the city represents public life, the place of opportunity: "You are the light of the world. A city built on a hill cannot be hidden . . . let your light shine before others" (Matt 5:14, 16).

The letter to the Hebrews presents Jesus as a pilgrim between earth and heaven, the pioneer and forerunner to heaven. "For here we have no lasting city, but we are looking for the city that is to come" (Heb 13:14). The heavenly Jerusalem is, in a true sense, our true home. As Paul puts it: "Our citizenship is in heaven" (Phil 3:20). The Bible ends with a vision of the heavenly Jerusalem and a loud voice crying from God's throne:

> And I saw the holy city, the new Jerusalem, coming down out of heaven from God, prepared as a bride adorned for her husband. And I heard a loud voice from the throne saying,
>
>> "See, the home of God is among mortals.
>> He will dwell with them as their God;
>> they will be his peoples,
>> and God himself will be with them. . . ."
>
> I saw no temple in the city, for its temple is the Lord God the Almighty and the Lamb. And the city has no need of sun or moon to shine on it, for the glory of God is its light, and its lamp is the Lamb. . . .
>
> Blessed are those who wash their robes, so that they will have the right to the tree of life and may enter the city by the gates. (Rev 21:2-3, 22-23; 22:14)

Christian hymnody celebrates this theme. Samuel Johnson (1822–82) exults:

> City of God, how broad and far
> Outspread thy walls sublime! . . .
>
> How grandly hath thine empire grown
> Of freedom , love, and truth![10]

With twelfth-century Bernard of Cluny we sing out:

> Jerusalem the Golden,
>> With milk and honey blest,

Beneath thy contemplation
  Sink heart and voice oppressed:
I know not, O I know not,
What social joys are there;
What radiancy of glory,
What light beyond compare![11]

As we reflect on what role the metaphor of the city might play in our lives, then, we realize that it represents both the experience of stress, conflict, noise, and demand, but it also becomes the symbol of our greatest hopes. The human city points to the heavenly abode. Despite the fact that Christianity developed principally as an urban movement, Christians have often preferred metaphors from the natural world, rather than from the human city.[12] What hints do we get from the great spiritual writers?

In the fifth century, Augustine of Hippo challenged Christians: do they want to live in the transient indulgences of the city of man or discover the eternal joys of the City of God?[13] In the sixteenth century, Ignatius of Loyola's *Spiritual Exercises* included a meditation on the Two Standards, in which two cities, Jerusalem and Babylon, are the sites where Christ and the evil one each gather their respective followers. On the one hand we are tempted to the path of avarice, pride, and status, while on the other we are summoned to the way of simplicity, humility, and vulnerability. Ignatius asks us: Which city will you chose? Where do you wish to stand?

The human city and the city of God can also represent the two kingdoms. Jesus proclaimed the kingdom of God in the midst of the kingdom of Rome, posing the question: What would life look like if God, not Caesar, was on the throne?[14] The reality we face each day is that we have dual citizenship. While we are called to live as responsible citizens of the human city, our lifestyle and values should be shaped by the kingdom and reign of God. This is precisely the dilemma and setting of the book of Revelation—the first Christians faced persecution under the tyranny of Roman oppression, while their hearts were set on heaven. The spiritual director or Christian supporting another in the spiritual life encounters time and again the conflict, strain, and tension of a person pulled in two opposite directions. We need to articulate the Gospel call to live within the kingdom of God while witnessing and serving here below. We need to return, again and again, to that greater vision, that sustains us and inspires us.

Another way of looking at our spiritual vocation is that we are pulled between the city and the desert, between engagement and solitude. But remember, you can see the threshold of the City of Jerusalem, the Mount of Olives, even when you are deep in the Judean desert!

Questions for Reflection and Discussion

1. What are you aiming at as a Christian? What are your plans? What do you hope will be your lasting legacy? Recall Hebrews 11:10: Abraham "looked forward to the city that has foundations, whose architect and builder is God." And recall Psalm 127:1: "Unless the LORD builds the house, those who build it labor in vain."

2. In what ways does your spiritual life resemble a construction site? Are there things that need to be torn down before something new emerges?

3. In what room do you find yourself, according to Teresa's *Interior Castle*? What is the next room beckoning you?

4. Is there any sense in your spiritual life that you have become trapped or restricted in some way? How does the imagery of opening doors or finding release resonate with your longings? Is there something in you that needs to be unlocked? Do you feel in any way "fastened up" or "zipped up" spiritually?

Further Reading

Nolan, Albert. *Jesus Today: A Spirituality of Radical Freedom*. Maryknoll, NY: Orbis, 2006.

Philippe, Jacques. *Interior Freedom*. New York: Scepter, 2007.

Wingate, Andrew. *Free to Be: Discovering the God of Freedom*. London: Darton, Longman & Todd, 2000.

8

The Sensuous Language of the Body

> "Late have I loved you, beauty so
> old and so new. . . . You were
> fragrant, and I drew in my breath
> and now I pant after you. I tasted
> you, and I feel but hunger and thirst
> for you. You touched me."
>
> — Saint Augustine, Confessions[1]

While the Hebrew Scriptures declare that creation is "very good," the Christian faith affirms that the divine Word became enfleshed and embodied, taking on human flesh and blood in the person of Jesus Christ. In the wake of the incarnation, physicality and spirituality become inseparable. This enables us to develop a Christian anthropology, essential for the practice of spiritual direction, that takes seriously both the human body and our capacity to welcome the divine, as we are made in the image and likeness of God (Gen 1:27). We encounter striking physical images: in the tenth century Simeon the New Theologian wrote of the need for one to have "purified his heart through repentance and many tears, and penetrated the depths of humility, and became pregnant with the Holy Spirit, by the grace and love for mankind of our Lord Jesus Christ."[2]

Here we explore seven themes: the heart, the spiritual senses, feeding, inebriation, spiritual nakedness, hurting/healing, and heaviness/lightness.

The Heart

The key symbol that expresses spiritual embodiment is the biblical symbol of the heart. As the *Catechism of the Catholic Church* reminds us: "According to Scripture, it is the *heart* that prays. . . . The heart is the dwelling-place where I am, where I live; according to the Semitic or biblical expression, the heart is the place 'to which I withdraw.' The heart is our hidden center. . . . the place of encounter, because as image of God we live in relation."[3] As Pope Benedict XVI puts it: "In biblical language, the 'heart' indicates the centre of human life, the point where reason, will, temperament and sensitivity converge, where the person finds his unity and his interior orientation."[4] According to the Hebraic tradition, the heart is the center of the human, uniting the intellectual, emotional, and volitional functions of the person.[5] It stands as a potent symbol of the inner life that is embodied and incarnate.

Communicating the ideals of monastic direction to the West, John Cassian (365–435) advocates purity of heart, a clear vision, a singleness of purpose, in relation to the spiritual life: "Every art and every discipline has a particular objective, that is to say, a target and an end particularly its own . . . the aim of our profession is the kingdom of God or the kingdom of heaven. But the point of reference, our objective, is a clean heart, without which it is impossible for anyone to reach our target."[6]

The "heart" image enables a dialogue between Eastern and Western Christian perspectives on prayer. Ware reminds us, in Orthodox theology: "the heart signifies the deep self; it is the seat of wisdom and understanding, the place where our moral decisions are made, the inner shrine in which we experience divine grace and the indwelling of the Holy Trinity. It indicates the human person as a 'spiritual subject,' created in God's image and likeness."[7] Ware goes on: "Here is no head–heart dichotomy, for the intellect is *within* the heart. The heart is the meeting point between body and soul, between the subconscious, conscious and supraconscious, between the human and the divine."[8] Abbot Ephraim reminds us: "St. John Damascene remarks that 'as the eyes are to the body, so the intellect is to the soul' . . . this function of the intellect is an internal insight."[9] Simeon the New Theologian writes of *moving* or relocating the mind to the heart: "The mind should be in the heart. . . . Keep your mind there (in the heart), trying by every possible means to find the place where the heart is, in order that, having found it, your mind should constantly abide there. Wrestling thus, your mind will find the place of the heart."[10]

If the Orthodox perspective emerges from a particular view of the human person, what kind of knowledge is to be sought? Maximos in the seventh century puts it: "When the intellect (*nous*) practices contemplation, it advances in spiritual knowledge . . . the intellect is granted the grace of theology when, carried on wings of love . . . it is taken up into God and with the help of the Holy Spirit discerns—as far as this is possible for the human intellect—the qualities of God."[11] Such knowledge is transforming: "The intellect joined to God for long periods through prayer and love becomes wise, good, powerful, compassionate, merciful and long-suffering; in short, it includes with itself almost all the divine qualities."[12]

The heart represents an awareness of the divine in a wide range of traditions. The writer of Ephesians had prayed: "with the eyes of your heart enlightened, you may know what is the hope to which he has called you, what are the riches of his glorious inheritance among the saints" (1:18). Augustine experienced an inner listlessness: "our hearts are restless til they rest in You." Benedict's Rule begins with the words "Listen carefully, my son, to the master's instructions, and attend to them with the ear of your heart" (RB Prol. 1). George Herbert's hymn invites us: "with a well tuned heart sing thou the songs of love," while Charles Wesley pens the great hymn beginning: "O for a heart to praise my God."

The Spiritual Senses

In his wonderful account of the risen Christ meeting the disciples on the road to Emmaus, Luke repeatedly uses the metaphor of spiritual sight: "But their eyes were kept from recognizing him. . . . They stood still, looking sad. . . . 'Some of those who were with us went to the tomb and found it just as the women had said; but they did not see him.' . . . Then their eyes were opened, and they recognized him; and he vanished from their sight" (Luke 24:16-17, 24, 31).

In the physicality of breaking bread together, they come to spiritual insight. Prayer enables an awakening of the spirit and the body: a coming fully alive, aware and responsive to what God wants to offer us. In prayer we seek fresh vision, wider perspective. Of course, we can also be blinkered and suffer from spiritual myopia. Ephrem (d. 373), the prolific and inspiring Syriac writer, encourages us in prayer to see reality differently, using his famed image of the "luminous eye," which can look into the hiddenness of God's mystery:

> Blessed is the person who has acquired a luminous eye
> With which he will see how much the angels stand in awe of You, Lord,
> And how audacious is man.[13]

Ephrem encourages us to pray for the gift of the inner eye, which penetrates the deep things of God and gives true insight. In this way our prayer can become luminous, radiant, and light revealing:

> Let our prayer be a mirror, Lord, placed before Your face;
> Then Your fair beauty will be imprinted on its luminous surface.[14]

In the fourth century Gregory of Nyssa wrote about the spiritual senses in his commentary on the Song of Songs:

> We have two sets of senses, one corporeal and the other spiritual, as the Word tells us in the book of Proverbs: "Thou shalt find the sense of God." There is a correspondence between the motions and movements of the soul and the sense organs of the body. . . . A kiss is an operation of the sense of touch: in a kiss two pairs of lips touch. There is, however, a spiritual faculty of touch, which comes in contact with the Word, and this is actuated by a spiritual and immaterial sense of touch, as it is said: "Our hands have handled, of the word of life" (1 John 1:1).[15]

In the thirteenth century, the Franciscan Bonaventure writes that prayer requires the rediscovery of the spiritual senses: "when the inner senses are restored to see the highest beauty, to hear the highest harmony, to smell the highest fragrance, to taste the highest sweetness, to apprehend the highest delight, the soul is prepared for spiritual ecstasy through devotion, admiration and exultation."[16] This is the invitation of prayer.

Ignatius of Loyola invites us to hone our spiritual sensibilities and activate our five senses within our imaginations as we engage with the text, especially when we read the episodes from the life of Christ in the Bible. Ignatius says to use your eyes to *look* at the scene, visualize it, imagine it in your mind's eye, place yourself into the picture, and become one of the characters. Reach out in your imagination and *touch* with your fingertips the characters, the soil, the water, and all of the physical aspects. Even *smell* the scents of the scene and *taste* the air, the food, and the atmosphere. But above all, Ignatius says, open your ears and *listen* to what the characters are saying to each other, what they are saying to you and what God is saying to you through all this. This approach to Scripture once again slows us down, demanding our time and attention. It leads to clearer discernment of God's will for us in the practice of ministry. That is the point: engagement with Word leads us to echo St. Ignatius's own prayer: "Take, O Lord, and receive my entire liberty, my memory, my understanding and my whole will. All that I am and all that I possess You have given me: I surrender it all to You to be disposed of according to Your will. Give me only Your love and Your grace; with these I will be rich enough."[17]

Feeding and Ingesting

Paul regularly resorts to the imagery of eating and feeding as he looks for metaphors of spiritual growth: "And so, brothers and sisters, I could not speak to you as spiritual people, but rather as people of the flesh, as infants in Christ. I fed you with milk, not solid food, for you were not ready for solid food. Even now you are still not ready, for you are still of the flesh" (1 Cor 3:1-3).

The theme of spiritual hunger and thirst is a recurrent one in the history of Christian spirituality. It relates to feeding both on Word and Sacrament. The soul is nourished and given sustenance as the banquet of the Eucharist empowers and energizes us. Jesus utilized this image: "Meanwhile the disciples were urging him, 'Rabbi, eat something.' But he said to them, 'I have food to eat that you do not know about.' So the disciples said to one another, 'Surely no one has brought him something to eat?' Jesus said to them, 'My food is to do the will of him who sent me and to complete his work'" (John 4:31-34). In our spiritual lives we become faint and weary. We do not always attend to our spiritual diet or intake. Sometimes we become malnourished. Jesus' words resound across the centuries: "I am the bread of life. Whoever comes to me will never be hungry, and whoever believes in me will never be thirsty" (John 6:35).

The discipline of *lectio divina*—the slow, ponderous, meditative reading of Scripture developed by Benedict and the monastic tradition—has been likened to "slow eating." There are four stages. First, *lectio* invites us to take a bite, reading a passage attentively, alert to particular words that strike us. Second, in *meditatio* we can hold the Word in our mind and heart as a piece of fruit might be held in the mouth: we take time to ask the Holy Spirit to lead us to its deepest meaning. Third, in *oratio* we savor its taste—bitter, sweet, or surprising—and allow this to lead us into a kind of prayer that dare ask questions of God: What are you saying? How might I have to change? In this phase, we expose our deepest needs and hopes. The Word will heal, disturb, and invigorate. Finally, in *contemplatio* we digest the Word, welcome the Word within our very selves, integrate it, interiorize it, and absorb it into our very being. One may need to practice this form of prayer over time in order to discover its depths. At first *lectio divina* may seem a busy way to pray, but with practice one can learn the art of "relishing the Word," releasing its power and energy into our lives.

Imbibing and Inebriation

The bridegroom in the Song of Songs calls out: "Eat, friends, drink, and be drunk with love" (5:1). And Paul writes: "Do not get drunk with wine . . . but be filled with the Spirit" (Eph 5:18). Gregory of Nyssa used the phrase "sober inebriation" to describe a spiritual ecstasy that comes from drinking in God's love in the chalice of the Eucharist and in the course of virtuous living. Macarius the Great spoke of being "intoxicated with God,"[18] while Isaac the Syrian (613–700) told of how God seizes the soul and leads the person into a state of divine madness, becoming a fool for Christ. In the Syriac, the term "inebriation" is linked linguistically to the term for "wonder" or "amazement":

> Sometimes . . . while prayer remains for its part, the intellect is taken away from it as if into heaven, and tears fall like fountains of waters, involuntarily soaking the whole face. All this time such a person is serene, still and filled with a wonder-filled vision. . . . he remains continually in amazement at God's work of creation—like people who are crazed by wine, for this is the "wine which causes the person's heart to rejoice" (Ps 104:15). . . . Blessed is the person who has entered this door in the experience of his own soul, for all the power of ink, letters and phrases is too feeble to indicate the delight of this mystery.[19]

Bernard of Clairvaux wrote of "that sober inebriation which comes not from drinking new wine but from enjoying God." Mechthild of Magdeburg in her *Flowing Light of the Godhead* delights in the heady brew of divine love: "God lays the soul in his glowing heart so that He, the great God, and she, the humble maid, embrace and are united as thoroughly as water is with wine."[20] In this "cup of blessing" we taste rich imagery expressing the way God's grace stimulates and arouses us. We forget our sorrows and rediscover the overwhelming joy of God.

Nakedness and Clothing

The imagery of stripping ourselves nude in a state of spiritual nakedness before God has been touched upon in chapter 6 when we considered the vulnerability represented by exposure in the wilderness. Indeed, from his fourth-century monastery at Bethlehem, Jerome put it: "The desert loves to strip bare."[21] Of course this resonates with the original baptismal liturgy, where the candidate removes his clothes at the water's edge, symbolizing the renunciation of the candidate's former life, and arising from the waters is clothed with a new white garment representing new life in Christ. It also recalls the story of St. Francis: he stripped off his rich clothes before his father (a cloth merchant) and bishop, a sign that he was leaving behind the self-indulgent life that they represented. Walking away naked depicted his discovery of radical freedom in Christ.

This imagery reverberates with us in many ways. We wish to "cover up" before God, to conceal our nakedness as did Adam in the garden of

Eden. Yet we sense that we must hide nothing before God, and we long to be enveloped, clothed, and even enshrouded by the love of Christ. We are enrobed and mantled with a new dignity in Christ. In the hymns and poems of Ephrem, Christ as the new Adam cloaks the old in a robe of glory: in baptism we are clothed in garments of light.[22] In the West, Julian of Norwich writes: "we are clad and enclosed in the great goodness of God." This theme reappears in the prayer offered in the Way of the Cross when we recall Christ stripped of his garments: "Grant to us that stripped of our vices and adorned with virtue we may deserve to be present in white garments before the tribunal of Your majesty."[23] It prompts us to ask: Is there any attitude or habit that needs stripping in my life? We echo the longing of Paul's letter to the Colossians: "Do not lie to one another, seeing that you have stripped off the old self with its practices and have clothed yourselves with the new self, which is being renewed in knowledge according to the image of its creator. . . As God's chosen ones, holy and beloved, clothe yourselves with compassion, kindness, humility, meekness, and patience" (Col 3:9-10, 12).[24]

Hurting and Healing

Rolheiser reminds us that all Christian spirituality is essentially paschal in character. He contrasts two types of death: a terminal death that ends possibilities and a paschal death that opens one up to a new future.[25] The theme of divine wounding has a long history.

The story of Jacob struggling with the angel in Genesis 32 powerfully symbolizes the imagery of divine wounding. Jacob's thigh is put out of joint as he wrestles with him (32:25), and Jacob is brought to a point of brokenness. His running symbolizes his independence, his desire to escape uncomfortable truths and conflicts, his evasion of God, and his determination to stay in control of his life. Such running and exhaustion resonates with the often self-inflicted stresses that are experienced in Christian life. Now Jacob can run no longer: now he can only limp, for God touches him and disables him. He is reduced to a state of new dependency on God. This wounding of Jacob represents God finally melting his willfulness and paralyzing his defiant ego. For the moment, at least, he crumples up—God has the mastery.

This language is taken up by John of the Cross, who begins his poem *The Spiritual Canticle*:

> Where have you hidden,
> Beloved, and left me moaning?

> You fled like the stag
> after wounding me;
> I went out calling you, but you were gone . . .
> Why, since you wounded
> this heart, don't you heal it?[26]

This resonates with a process of radical dispossession that John of the Cross sees at the center of prayer's movement from egocentricity to God-centeredness, a process in which God seeks to reshape us and convert the ego. The renunciation of one's own confidences enables a total surrender to God: the pain to be faced is that of being stripped of our egotistical powers. As Follent puts it: "The abandonment of self-mastery and the taking on of a radical dependence on God will necessarily be accompanied by a sense of being undone or being annihilated, yet such an anxiety is quite ungrounded. In fact, the discovery that one can no longer find one's guarantees in oneself may indeed be a sign that progress in the life with God is finally being achieved."[27]

John's contemporary Teresa of Avila described her experience of God in terms of a divine wounding. In Rome's church of Santa Maria della Vittoria one can see Bernini's great sculpture *The Ecstasy of Saint Teresa*, her heart pierced by a divine arrow of love, which was inspired by her words:

> The pain was so severe that it made me utter several moans. The sweetness caused by this intense pain is so extreme that one cannot possibly wish it to cease, nor is one's soul then content with anything but God. This is not a physical, but a spiritual pain, though the body has some share in it—even a considerable share. So gentle is this wooing which takes place between the soul and God.[28]

Rowan Williams entitles his book on historical spirituality *The Wound of Knowledge*. The physicality of this metaphor denotes the pain and hurt involved in prayer—the cost of discipleship—the crucifixion of the ego. In the Celtic tradition, Columbanus (543–615) had offered this prayer: "Wound our souls with your love . . . for by love am I wounded, I desire that those wounds may be in me O Lord."[29] We ache for more of God in our lives.

The ancient Syriac tradition delights in imagery for the spiritual life with medical qualities. Ephrem calls the Eucharist the medicine of life that brings renewal and healing.[30] Christ is often called the physician and healer of souls by such writers as Aphrahat and Addai (see Matt 9:12); it is Ephrem's favorite title for Christ.[31] His anointing Spirit brings balm to sickness in the soul, and penance brings relief from the poisons of sin.

Heaviness and Lightness

A range of metaphors derives from the experience of carrying heavy weights. Psalm 42:11 asks: "Why are you cast down, O my soul, and why are you disquieted within me?" Jesus calls out: "Come to me, all you that are weary and are carrying heavy burdens, and I will give you rest" (Matt 11:28). The writer of Hebrews recognizes how unnecessary clutter slows us down in the spiritual race: "Therefore, since we are surrounded by so great a cloud of witnesses, let us also lay aside every weight and the sin that clings so closely, and let us run with perseverance the race that is set before us, looking to Jesus the pioneer and perfecter of our faith" (Heb 12:1). When we stumble and fall, trip and crash to the ground, we heed his words of encouragement: "Therefore lift your drooping hands and strengthen your weak knees, and make straight paths for your feet, so that what is lame may not be put out of joint, but rather be healed" (Heb 12:12-13). We need to decisively let go of our grip of the weight, as John Bunyan's *Pilgrim's Progress* puts it:

> Christian asked Mr. Goodwill if he would remove the burden from his back, for he was still carrying it and could by no means get it off without help. . . . Just as he came to the cross, his burden came loose, dropped from his shoulders, and went tumbling down the hill. It fell into an open grave, and I saw it no more.[32]

In contemporary worship, the song "I Am a New Creation," by Dave Bilbrough, celebrates "a lightness in my spirit."[33] There is an exhilarating sense of release and liberation: "no more in condemnation." The heavy weight of guilt, shame, or sorrow, rather than becoming an impediment, drops away.

Stephen Cherry in his *Barefoot Prayers* sums up the use of body language in "A Monday Morning Prayer":

> Give me, this day,
> A lung full of spirit,
> An eye full of beauty,
> A step full of joy,
> A mouth full of praise,
> And hands full of nothing
> But desire to do your will. [34]

Questions for Reflection and Discussion

1. How comfortable are you in using physical and visceral images to speak of the spiritual life?

2. What is your experience of being wounded by God ?

3. What do you understand by the idea that in prayer we become "fully alive"?

4. How would you develop the theme of spiritual thirst and hunger to describe your own experience of finding God? "Taste and see that the LORD is good" (Ps 38:8). What does God taste like for you? Then look up Ps 119:103 for one response to this.

5. "'Come,' my heart says, 'seek his face!' Your face, LORD, do I seek" (Ps 27:8). How would you describe the face of God as you experience it in your prayer?

Further Reading

Fox, Matthew. *Creation Spirituality: Liberating Gifts for the Peoples of the Earth.* San Francisco: Harper, 1991.

Kubicki, James. *A Heart on Fire: Rediscovering Devotion to the Sacred Heart of Jesus.* Notre Dame, IN: Ave Maria, 2012.

Newell, J. Philip. *Echo of the Soul: The Sacredness of the Human Body.* Norwich: Canterbury, 2000.

9

The Archetypal Language of the Elements

O wondrous God
O God of the earth,
O God of fire,
O God of the excellent waters,
O God of the tempestuous and
   rushing air . . .
O God of the waves from the
   bottomless house of the ocean . . .
Have mercy upon us.

– Attributed to Mugrón,
   Abbot of Iona[1]

This litany, from a tenth-century abbot of the famed monastery of Iona, introduces us to an encounter with three primordial metaphors of the Spirit drawn from the elements at work in creation: wind, fire, and water. In this chapter we will note how these themes are developed in hymnody ancient and modern. Later, we will explore darkness and cloud in our last chapter.

Wind

At the dawn of creation, Genesis tells us, the wind of God blew over the primal chaos of the waters. Human life began when God breathed into the nostrils of man the breath of life—the *ruach*—and "man became a living being" (Gen 2:7). Into the valley of dry bones God speaks: "Look, I will cause breath to enter into you, and you shall live" (Ezek 37:5).

At Pentecost (Acts 2) the Spirit of God as a "mighty wind" blows into the Christian community. Was it a gentle breeze or a stormy gale? What type of wind buffeting Jerusalem does Luke have in mind? The cooling afternoon breeze that blows in from the Mediterranean, bringing refreshment? The dry scorching Hamseen wind from the south that unsettles? The stormy winter wind that comes as the harbinger of spring, turning back the drought and enabling new shoots? At various points in our lives, the Holy Spirit will come to us differently. We may not predict the moving of the wind in our spiritual lives but we must expose ourselves to its presence: "the wind blows where it chooses, and you hear the sound of it, but you do not know where it comes from or where it goes. So it is with everyone who is born of the Spirit" (John 3:8). As spiritual directors and soul friends, we need to have the sensitivity and courage to read what is going on in the other person, and to detect and interpret the clues and evidences: whether they are ready to move ahead in some way, whether it is time to hoist the sails, catch the wind and follow the leading of the Spirit—or whether it is time to take cover!

At the close of the Fourth Gospel, as the risen Christ appears in the Upper Room "he breathed on them and said, 'Receive the Holy Spirit' (John 20:22). The nineteenth-century English theologian Edwin Hatch celebrates this metaphor in his well-known hymn:

> Breathe on me, breath of God,
> Fill me with life anew,
> That I may love what Thou dost love,
> And do what Thou wouldst do.[2]

Gerard Manley Hopkins develops the metaphor in daring ways in his poem "The Blessed Virgin Compared to the Air We Breathe." He calls her

> Wild air, world-mothering air,
> Nestling me everywhere.

Wind—and air—become powerful images of God's providence and mysterious presence.

Fire

Fire denotes the mysterious and energizing divine presence of a theophany: the burning bush that calls Moses to his liberating vocation (Exod 3:2) and the awesome appearance of God atop Mount Sinai: "Now Mount Sinai was wrapped in smoke because the Lord had descended on it in fire. The smoke of it went up like the smoke of a kiln, and the whole mountain trembled greatly" (Exod 19:18). The divine fire falls on Elijah's sacrifice atop Mount Carmel (1 Kgs 18:38), consuming the offering. But the fire of the Old Testament is not only an outer visible conflagration. Jeremiah speaks of an *inner* flame, a divine compulsion: "If I say, 'I will not mention him, or speak any more in his name,' there is in my heart as it were a burning fire shut up in my bones, and I am weary with holding it in, and I cannot" (Jer 20:9).

Shockingly, Jesus cries out in the gospels: "I came to cast fire on the earth, and would that it were already kindled!" (Luke 12:49). The writer to the Hebrews warns us: "Our God is a consuming fire" (12:29). Fire often denotes and symbolizes the Holy Spirit; Luke describes his advent in terms of "divided tongues as of fire appeared to them and rested on each one of them" (Acts 2:23). Paul exhorts the Romans to "be aglow with the Spirit" (12:11), and to Timothy he writes: "For this reason I remind you to rekindle the gift of God that is within you through the laying on of my hands" (2 Tim 1:6).

In the rich heritage of the Syriac spiritual tradition, St. Ephrem, poet, hymnwriter, and deacon, gives us an outstanding example in his great *Hymn on Faith:*

> See, Fire and Spirit are in the womb of her who bore You;
> See, Fire and Spirit are in the river in which You were baptized.
> Fire and Spirit are in our baptismal font,
> In the Bread and the Cup are Fire and Holy Spirit.[3]

Two fourteenth-century writers in particular delight in the imagery of fire.

The English mystic Richard Rolle (1300–1349) opens his treatise *The Fire of Love* with the arresting words: "I cannot tell you how surprised I was the first time I felt my heart begin to warm. It was a real warmth too not imaginary, and it felt as if it were actually on fire. . . . But once I realized that it came entirely from within, that this fire of love had no cause, material or sinful, but was the gift of my Maker, I was absolutely delighted."[4] Rolle extols, with unbridled enthusiasm, the affective dimensions of Christian spirituality; he also describes the experience of God in terms of music, sweetness, and light.[5]

The Italian seer Catherine of Siena (1347–80) writes of the imagery of fire in a very powerful way:

> You know the only thing that can bind a person is a bond; the only way to become one with the fire is to throw oneself into it that not a bit of oneself remains outside it. . . . Once we are in its embrace, the fire of divine charity does to our soul what physical fire does; it warms us, enlightens us, changes us into itself. Oh gentle and fascinating fire! You warm and you can drive out all the cold of vice and

sin and self-centeredness! This heat so warms and enkindles the dry wood of our will that it bursts into flame and swells in tender loving desires, loving what God loves and hating what God hates. And I tell you, once we see ourselves so boundlessly loved, and see how the slain lamb has given himself on the wood of the cross, the fire floods us with light, leaving no room for darkness. So enlightened by that venerable fire, our understanding expands and opens wide. For the light from the fire lets us see that everything (except sin and vice) comes from God. . . . Once your understanding has received the light from the fire as I've described, the fire transforms you into itself and you become one with the fire. . . How truly then we can say that he is a fire who warms and enlightens and transforms us into himself!⁶

In the sixteenth century John of the Cross (1542–91) delights in the image of a human log becoming radiant in the divine flame: "We can compare the soul in . . . this state of transformation of love to the log of wood that is ever immersed in fire, and the acts of this soul to the flame that blazes up from the fire of love. The more intense the fire of union, the more vehemently does this fire burst into flames." It is a blending of fires human and divine, for John notes: "Such is the activity of the Holy Spirit in the soul transformed by love: The interior acts he produces shoot up flames, for they are acts of inflamed love, in which the will of the soul united with that flame, made one with it, loves most sublimely."

The divine flame cauterizes the soul, and at once heals and pains, as we saw in the last chapter's theme of the divine wounding:

> O living flame of love
> That tenderly wounds my soul
> In its deepest center!⁷

Hymns of Fire

This imagery is developed in hymnody, ancient and modern. Charles Wesley provides an awesome vision of the divine life touching us:

> O Thou Who camest from above,
> The pure celestial fire to impart,
> Kindle a flame of sacred love
> Upon the mean altar of my heart.
> There let it for Thy glory burn
> With inextinguishable blaze,
> And trembling to its source return,

In humble prayer and fervent praise.
Jesus, confirm my heart's desire
To work and speak and think for Thee;
Still let me guard the holy fire,
And still stir up Thy gift in me.[8]

Indeed, in his journals his brother John had described his conversion experience in terms of "my heart felt strangely warmed," evoking the road to Emmaus: "Did not our hearts burn within us?" (Luke 24:32). In our own time, this archetypal language continues to resonate in our souls, as the English singer-songwriter Graham Kendrick prays, "Blaze, Spirit blaze, Set our hearts on fire!" and the Australian David Evans sings, "He burns with holy fire, with splendor he is crowned." So what does it mean? The divine fire denotes three aspects of God's activity within us.

First, it alludes to God's purifying work in us: "For he is like a refiner's fire and like fullers' soap; he will sit as a refiner and purifier of silver, and he will purify the descendants of Levi and refine them like gold and silver, until they present offerings to the LORD in righteousness" (Mal 3:2-3). Fire destroys and consumes the dross that rises to the surface when metals are liquefied. This evokes the fire of judgment of the apocalyptic prophet John the Baptist: "the chaff he will burn with unquenchable fire" (Matt 3:12). Isaiah experiences a cleansing flame in the temple: the angel takes a burning coal to the lips of Isaiah—this represents a deep experience: guilt is taken away and Isaiah hears God's call: "Who will go for us?" (Isa 6:8).

A second theme is the empowering, energizing presence of God in us. The divine fire is kindled within us, illuminating our way and causing us to shine out with inextinguishable love—we are called to irradiate divine love, to be incandescent. Even our words are set aflame:

Catch the flash-over,
A wordage set alight,
Instantaneous combustion,
Our talking like blazes.
Flamboyance of speech.
A spirited discussion.
Our words flaring up
. . . .
Tongues of fire.[9]

A third theme celebrates the infectious, contagious character of the divine fire blazing in us. Each Easter, from the darkness of the cave-tomb of Christ, Holy Fire breaks out in Jerusalem's Basilica of the Resurrection.

In the gloom of the tomb each Holy Saturday, a new light is kindled. It is passed out and quickly spread among thousands of pilgrims, each of whom has a bundle of thirty-three candles representing the earthly life of Christ. The Holy Fire spreads like wildfire as the tapers become a radiant torch. The darkness is overcome and dispelled; the whole basilica is filled not only with light but with fire, which is rushed out onto the streets of Jerusalem, and taken by runners to Christians living behind the Separation Barrier in the West Bank and by plane to Greece and Russia. The Holy Fire is a powerful symbol that the darkness cannot quench the light of Christ, that the life and hope of the risen One is an inextinguishable blaze. As the Orthodox liturgy for Easter puts it:

> Now are all things filled with light;
> Heaven and earth, and the nethermost regions of the earth![10]

In a memorable episode from the desert fathers we learn the soul's true potential:

> Abba Lot went to see Abba Joseph and said to him, "Abba, as far as I can I say my little office, I fast a little, I pray and meditate, I live in peace and as far as I can, I purify my thoughts. What else can I do?" Then the old man stood up and stretched his hands towards heaven. His fingers became like ten lamps of fire and he said to him, "If you will, you can become all flame."[11]

Our potential and vocation is to be ignited by the Spirit, engulfed with his fire, radiant and ablaze with the Spirit himself, the divine flame.

Though we do not encounter raw fire as our ancestors did each day in the hearth, we may recall for ourselves contemporary usages. We might be pointed to industry: the crucible, holding molten metal.[12] More commonly we may witness fire in the fields, which may at first sight alarm us, until we realize its healing potential: after harvest time, a field may be scorched by flame in order to burn off stubble, return goodness to the soil, and encourage new growth.

Water

Water has become an evocative symbol of the spiritual life. The Bible begins and closes with rivers of water, bespeaking creation and new creation: "a stream would rise from the earth and water the whole face of the ground, then the Lord God formed man. . . . a river flows out of Eden to water the garden" (Gen 2:6-7, 10; cf. 1:1). In the Apocalypse "the

Lamb will guide them to the springs of the water of life" (Rev 7:17), and the vision concludes: "Then the angel showed me the river of the water of life, bright as crystal, flowing from the throne of God and of the Lamb through the middle of the street of the city. On either side of the river is the tree of life . . . producing its fruit each month; and the leaves of the tree are for the healing of the nations" (Rev 22:1-2).

Baptism reminds us of the need to be flooded, engulfed, drenched, and saturated by the waters of the Holy Spirit. Throughout our spiritual life we need the overflowing, inundating Spirit to irrigate the parched earth of our soul. Streams of grace need to percolate the soul. As Paul puts it: "God's love has been poured into our hearts through the Holy Spirit that has been given to us" (Rom 5:5). We pray with Hosea:

> Let us know, let us press on to know the LORD;
>   his appearing is as sure as the dawn;
> he will come to us like the showers,
>   like the spring rains that water the earth. (Hos 6:3)

Sometimes we will cry out with the prophet Amos:

> [L]et justice roll down like waters,
>   and righteousness like an ever-flowing stream. (5:24)

Hidden Streams and Rivers

The mystery of prayer can indeed be represented by the image of a river. The river is at once a primordial and eschatological image of the divine life.[13] Like a hidden spring or underground river, prayer is often unseen and unrecognized, elusive but having powerful influences. Prayer as a secret river remains something that cannot be measured or quantified. It is something essentially mysterious, but rises to the surface and reveals its presence in a number of different expressions. As Roose-Evans puts it: "This secret life with God is like an underground river . . . we cannot see it, but we know it is there. Like water diviners we sense its presence within ourselves and also in others. We know it is there, even though others may doubt and challenge its reality. God is an underground river flowing to the sea. . . . The underground river flows through each one of us."[14]

The river is an image that reflects diversity and flexibility. Rivers have different characteristics as they flow through the terrain, from incisive fast-flowing torrents to meandering ponderous currents; likewise, prayer goes through various phases and embraces different intensities. The diversity of prayer encompasses turbulence and confusion, as well as contemplative peace. As a river will course through different geologies (the great biblical river of the Jordan itself flowing along a fault line) so prayer will encounter both resistance and weakness.

"There is a river whose streams make glad the city of God" (Ps 46:4). The image of water in the Scriptures is predominantly concerned not with cleansing but with giving life, often associated with the work of the Holy Spirit. In John's gospel we are led to Jacob's well, a symbol of humanity's thirst. Jesus says: "If you knew the gift of God . . . you would have asked him and he would have given you living water . . . . Those who drink of the water that I will give them will never be thirsty. The water that I will give will become in them a spring of water gushing up to eternal life" (4:10, 14). Jesus promises a Spirit who quenches our deepest thirst, an inner geyser, welling up to eternal life. The woman represents all of humanity in her cry: "Sir, give me this water" (John 4:15). As the twelfth-century Armenian poet Nerses Shnorhali puts it:

> O Fountain of life, you asked for water from the woman of Samaria,
> And promised her living water,
> in return for the transitory one.
> Grant to me, O Fountain of Life,
> That holy drink for my soul,
> That flows from the heart in rivers,
> The Spirit from whom grace gushes forth.[15]

The seventh chapter of John's gospel proclaims the dramatic cry of Christ:

> On the last day of the festival, the great day, while Jesus was standing there, he cried out, "Let anyone who is thirsty come to me, and let the one who believes in me drink. As the scripture has said, 'Out of the believer's heart shall flow rivers of living water.'" Now he said this about the Holy Spirit . . . which believers in him were to receive, for as yet there was no Spirit, because Jesus was not yet glorified. (John 7:37-39)

The great Jewish festival of Tabernacles, with its vision of the river of God, forms the context of this event. Jesus attends the temple liturgy where Ezekiel's vision (Ezek 47) was proclaimed to the pilgrims: a spring of God's generous blessing bursts forth from under the altar of the temple and it spills out to bring renewal to the whole world. In the glorious promise of the river of God Jesus suggests three steps the disciples need to take: "If anyone thirsts, let them come to me and drink. Out of their heart will flow rivers of living water." We first acknowledge and recognize our thirst for the Spirit. Second, we come to Jesus the giver of the Spirit and place ourselves in expectant relation to him. Third, we are invited to drink and receive afresh the living water. In our prayer we can take these three steps: we thirst, come to Jesus, and drink afresh of the Spirit of God.

In the history of Christian spirituality the image of water has inspired countless teachers of prayer. Let us look at two examples, drawn from East and West.

Springs and Fountains

Saint Symeon the New Theologian (949–1022) is one the Eastern church's greatest mystics. He emphasizes the necessity of personal encounter with the divine. As he tells his own story:

> He led me by the hand as one leads a blind man to the fountain head, that is, to the holy scriptures and to Your divine command-ments. . . . One day when I was hurrying to plunge myself in this daily bath, You met me on the road, You who had already drawn me out of the mire. Then for the first time the pure light of Your divine face shone before my weak eyes. . . . From that day on, You returned often at the fountain source, You would plunge my head into the water, letting me see the splendor of Your light. . . . One day when it seemed as though You were plunging me over and over again in the lustral waters, lightening flashes surrounded me. I saw the rays from Your face merge with the waters; washed by these radiant waters, I was carried out of myself.[16]

For Symeon, the image of the waters becomes a powerful metaphor of the spiritual life, bespeaking the unfathomable resources of the Spirit and God's generosity in sharing his gifts. In the West, St. Teresa of Avila confesses: "I cannot find anything more apt for the explanation of certain spiritual things than this element of water; for, as I am ignorant and my wit gives me no help and I am so fond of this element, I have looked at it more attentively than at other things."[17] She writes of a "prayer of quiet" using the picture of the fountain:

> Let us suppose that we are looking at two fountains, the basins of which can be filled with water. . . . These two large basins can be filled with water in different ways: the water in the one comes from a long distance, by means of numerous conduits and through human skill; but the other has been constructed at the very source of the water and fills without making any noise. If the flow of water is abun-dant, as in the case we are speaking of, a great stream still runs from it after it has been filled; no skill is necessary here, and no conduits

have to be made, for the water is flowing all the time. The difference between this and the carrying of the water by means of conduits is, I think, as follows. The latter corresponds to the spiritual sweetness which, as I say, is produced by meditation. It reaches us by way of the thoughts; we meditate upon created things and fatigue the understanding; and when at last, by means of our own efforts, it comes, the satisfaction which it brings to the soul fills the basin, but in doing so makes a noise, as I have said.

To the other fountain the water comes direct from its source, which is God, and, when it is His Majesty's will and He is pleased to grant us some supernatural favor, its coming is accompanied by the greatest peace and quietness and sweetness within ourselves.[18]

In this passage from the *Interior Castle*, written in 1577, Teresa suggests that there are two ways of receiving the water of God. Either we can stand at a distance from the fountain of God and receive the water of the Spirit as it were mediated through man-made and lengthy aqueducts and conduits, miles of pipelines of active, often noisy, talkative prayer (this in fact creates a distance from the fountain) or we can stand very close to the fountain of God, quieten our spirit, and change our prayer from an active thinking and striving style to a more receptive, passive, "drinking-in" style. In what Teresa calls the "prayer of quiet," we can drink directly and immediately of the river of the Spirit bubbling up in front of us. How close, she asks, are you to the fountain?

In his hymn "Glorious Things of Thee Are Spoken," John Newton puts it:

> See the streams of living waters,
> Springing from eternal love,
> Well supply thy sons and daughters,
> And all fear of want remove;
> Who can faint, while such a river
> Ever flows their thirst t'assuage?
> Grace which, like the Lord, the giver,
> Never fails from age to age.[19]

Dark Waters

Water is a double-edged symbol. As we noted in chapter five, it can denote death and danger, but it can also become the sign of salvation. The mystic John of the Cross describes the changes that can take place in prayer through the image of "dark water." From his prison in the Toledo city walls, John could hear few sounds but the rushing waters of the Tagus

River below.[20] This became an image to communicate the mysterious way in which God flows into human prayer: *"He made darkness and the dark water his hiding place* (Ps 18:10-11). . . . This darkness . . . and . . . the dark water of his dwelling denote the obscurity of faith in which he is enclosed."[21] The darkness refers to a process of radical dispossession that John sees at the heart of prayer's movement from egocentricity to God-centeredness, a process in which God seeks to reshape us and convert the ego.

Sometimes the spiritual life feels as if we find ourselves in a tempest. We are buffeted to and fro; we feel insecure and unsure of ourselves. We might join the evangelical Priscilla J. Owens in the words of her 1882 hymn:

> We have an anchor that keeps the soul
> Steadfast and sure while the billows roll,
> Fastened to the Rock which cannot move,
> Grounded firm and deep in the Savior's love.

> It is safely moored, 'twill the storm withstand,
> For 'tis well secured by the Savior's hand;
> And the cables, passed from His heart to mine,
> Can defy that blast, thro' strength divine.[22]

The Ocean of God

John Mason's hymn celebrates God's greatness:

> How great a being, Lord, is thine . . .
> Thy knowledge is the only line
> To sound so vast a deep.
> Thou art a sea without a shore.[23]

Faber developed this theme:

> There's a wideness in God's mercy
> like the wideness of the sea[24]

The thirteenth-century mystic Meister Eckhart invites us to discover the depths of the ocean of God:

> Think of the soul as a vortex or a whirlpool
>   And you will understand how we are to

Sink
  eternally
    from negation
      to negation
        into the one.
And how we are to
Sink
  eternally
    from letting go
      to letting go
        into God.[25]

Delighting in the imagery of sea and lake he goes on:

> The highest work of God is compassion.
>   And this means that God sets the soul
> in the highest and purest place which it can occupy:
> in space,
> in the sea,
> in a fathomless ocean,
> and there
> God works compassion.[26]

Mixing the Metaphors

Exposure to the elements was central to the experience of the Celtic Christians, who had lively traditions of *peregrination* and voyaging on the rough seas around Ireland and Scotland. They were motivated by a desire both to spread the Gospel and to discover God's providence in the deep, as depicted in the sixth-century *Voyage of Brendan.* The Celtic tradition brings together the elemental metaphors speaking of divine and human:

> *God*
> I am the wind that breathes upon the sea,
> I am the wave on the ocean,
> I am the murmur of leaves rustling,
> I am the rays of the sun.
>
> *The soul*
> I am a flame of fire, blazing with passionate love;
> I am a spark of light, illuminating the deepest truth...
> I am a wild storm, raging at human sins;
> I am a gentle breeze, blowing hope in the saddened heart.[27]

In his *Holy Sonnets* John Donne (1572–1631) also brings together these metaphors in a memorable mix:

> I am a little world made cunningly
> Of elements and an angelic sprite,
> But black sin hath betray'd to endless night
> My world's both parts, and oh both parts must die.
> You which beyond that heaven which was most high
> Have found new spheres, and of new lands can write,
> Pour new seas in mine eyes, that so I might
> Drown my world with my weeping earnestly,
> Or wash it, if it must be drown'd no more.
> But oh it must be burnt; alas the fire
> Of lust and envy have burnt it heretofore,
> And made it fouler; let their flames retire,
> And burn me O Lord, with a fiery zeal
> Of thee and thy house, which doth in eating heal.[28]

Questions for Reflection and Discussion

1. Fire: What is your experience of the divine fire? Dare you allow yourself to be singed—or *scorched*—by it? How would you use this in spiritual direction, or in talking with an enquirer about the difference that God makes in our lives? What ignites your spiritual life?

2. Water: How would you describe the meeting or quenching of your greatest inner thirsts? What is your experience of the spiritual storm?

3. Breath: On what sort of occasions do you find yourself longing for divine empowering? When do you feel God's breath?

Further Reading

Brock, Sebastian P. *The Syriac Fathers on Prayer and the Spiritual Life.* Kalamazoo, MI: Cistercian, 1987.

King, Angela, and Susan Clifford, ed. *The Rivers' Voice: An Anthology of Poetry.* Totnes, Devon: Green Books, 2000.

10

The Challenging Language of Struggle

> Batter my heart, three-person'd
> God . . .
> Overthrow me, and bend
> Your force, to break, blow, burn
> and make me new
>
> —John Donne, Holy Sonnets [1]

A significant cluster of metaphors for describing our relationship with God involves the language of struggling: the spiritual *combat*.[2] In chapter 5, we started to look at the theme of resistance in the spiritual life. It is normally a positive sign that something is happening when we sense a resistance or struggle. It takes us back to Gethsemane where Jesus moves from terror to trust and from hesitation to submission; here the garden becomes a spiritual battlefield where Jesus struggles with his destiny and with the call to suffering. He comes to the place of utter surrender, unreserved yielding to the divine will, and a total "giving in" to God—which of course opens the way to victory! While we may not take to such militaristic images as those in Ephesians 6:10-17 ("For our struggle is not against enemies of blood and flesh. . . . Take up the whole armor of God"), we recall that Timothy was called to "fight the good fight" (1 Tim 6:12), and the language of struggle or spiritual conflict sometimes needs to be part of our experience. As Charles Wesley puts it:

> Soldiers of Christ, arise,
> and put your armor on,
> strong in the strength which God supplies,
> through his eternal Son . . .
> From strength to strength go on,
> wrestle and fight and pray;

> tread all the powers of darkness down,
> and win the well-fought day.[3]

In the Celtic tradition there emerged prayers of *protection* such as St. Patrick's Breastplate—also known as the *lorica*—a prayer that rejoices in power of the Trinity to protect against foes without or within. Celtic Christians also use a *caim*, or encircling prayer, drawing an arc around them in the air to guard them from spiritual or physical attack.

Wrestling with God

The story of Jacob's wrestling with God in the swirling waters of the Jabbok (Gen 32:22-32) has become symbolic of the struggle of prayer. From the outset, as von Rad notes, the story was archetypal and representative: "It contains experiences of faith that extend from the most ancient period down to the time of the narrator . . . as it is now related it is clearly transparent as a type of that which Israel experienced from time to time with God."[4] It is the struggle of humanity with God. Jacob wrestled and fought with a Stranger, an unknown figure; he later described this encounter as saying "I have seen God face to face." It was indeed a divine–human combat.

Amidst the swirling currents Jacob experiences a barrier or frontier becoming a threshold or place of transition.[5] When seen as an encounter with God, this story casts light on the experience of prayer in formation because it is precisely in the waters of struggle, in the darkness, and in the experience of being wounded by God that Jacob receives his new name and new identity. No longer is he "Grasper" (Jacob) but "One who struggles with God" (Israel). This profound affirmation comes in the midst of solitude: "Jacob was left alone" (Gen 32:24). For Jacob this meant a letting go of attachments to people and possessions and standing alone before God. Prayer becomes a place of honesty and naked exposure to God, a place of risk and vulnerability where God is allowed both to wound and to bless. Henri Nouwen put it: "Solitude is thus the place of purification and transformation, the place of the great struggle and the great encounter. Solitude . . . is the place where Christ remodels us in his own image and frees us from the victimizing compulsions of the world. Solitude is the place of salvation."[6]

In giving Jacob a new identity God affirms the role of struggling in an evolving relationship with him. It is not to be avoided but faced: those who embrace their struggles with God can emerge with a clearer sense of identity and mission. Jacob's experience in the dark waters actually equips him to face the next stage of his journey. The torrent of prayer is experienced as a place of profound growth, and we become wounded healers: "For a deep understanding of our own pain makes it possible for us to convert our weakness into strength and to offer our own experience as source of healing."[7] As Brueggemann puts it, noting the significance of Jacob's struggle for ministry: "This narrative reflects some of Israel's most sophisticated theology. . . . God is God. . . . Jacob is a cripple with a blessing. . . . This same theology of weakness in power and power in weakness turns this text towards the New Testament and the gospel of the cross."[8]

George Herbert

> There thou art struggling with a peevish heart,
> Which sometimes crosseth thee, thou sometimes it:
> The fight is hard on either part.
> Great God doth fight. (Sion)[9]

Prayer is the place where we can bring to God the trials, joys, questions, and paradoxes of ministry. We come before God in our fragility and vulnerability, and in our brokenness, and we surrender to him the woes and heartaches of ministry for him to touch and transfigure. Thus all the struggles of ministry flow into prayer, which becomes a place of inner transformation by the Holy Spirit. Thus renewed, we are ready for the second movement of prayer, as we return to the world and to ministry reenergized, reinvigorated by God. George Herbert will help us look at these processes. In his poem "Prayer I" Herbert employs a range of vivid metaphors to communicate the wonder of prayer:

> Prayer the Church's banquet, angels' age,
> God's breath in man returning to his birth,
> The soul in paraphrase, heart in pilgrimage,
> The Christian plummet sounding heaven and earth;
> Engine against the Almighty, sinners' tower,
> Reversed thunder, Christ-side-piercing spear,
> The six-days-world-transposing in an hour,
> A kind of tune, which all things hear and fear;
> Softness, and peace, and joy, and love, and bliss,
> Exalted manna, gladness of the best,
> Heaven in ordinary, man well dressed,
> The milky way, the bird of paradise,
> Church-bells beyond the stars heard, the soul's blood,
> The land of spices; something understood.[10]

Certain phrases stand out:

> *The soul in paraphrase*—putting into words, expressing before God the longings of the spirit
>
> *heart in pilgrimage*—a sense that we might move, go places with God in prayer, or even change!
>
> *Engine against th' Almighty*—a siege engine throwing our feelings at God

The Anglican poet-priest of the seventeenth century George Herbert wrote that his poems were "a picture of the many spiritual conflicts that have passed betwixt God and my soul."[11] His poems testify to an ongoing struggle to accept personally within himself God's unconditional love. Herbert was born in 1593 to an aristocratic family. After studies at Cambridge University he became a lecturer in rhetoric and for seven years held the prestigious post of public orator to the university. He seemed destined for high office and set his hopes on a privileged career in the royal court, but God had other plans for him. Secular ambitions wrestled with a persistent and nagging sense of vocation to the priesthood, and Herbert finally gave in and was ordained deacon in 1626. But things were not to be straightforward for him. Illness and indecision delayed Herbert from entering full-time ministry, and he was not ordained priest until 1630. Some of Herbert's most poignant and questioning poems were composed during these four "wilderness" years. Herbert found himself appointed to a small and undistinguished parish church at Bemerton near Salisbury, to a vicarage in a state of disrepair.

For just three years he was to exercise his ministry—until his death in 1633. He embraced the life of a parish priest with extraordinary devotion and dedication, expressing his ideals for pastoral ministry in his work *The Country Parson.* He even found it possible to provide a place in his home for three orphaned nieces, even though he was on greatly reduced means. But he faced different struggles during this period. He no longer fought against his vocation but, dogged with ill health, found himself questioning his usefulness. Though he valued the presence of Christ in the Scriptures and in the sacraments, he wrestled with a sense of spiritual confusion and the dilemma of unanswered prayer, and he found himself echoing the sentiments of Jeremiah and the psalmists.

It is instructive to set *The Country Parson* alongside Herbert's poetry. In *The Country Parson* we see the ideal of parish ministry—that for which the minister should aim, the highest standards of pastoral care, preaching, study, home life, and even dealing with church wardens. But in his poems we glimpse the reality, the struggle, the heartache, and the *angst* of ministry—and how Herbert comes to terms with this, making sense of it all.

In *Affliction I* he tells the story of his spiritual journey:

> When first thou didst entice to thee my heart,
>   I thought the service brave

He experienced a time of happiness in God's service:

> What pleasures could I want, whose King I served,
>   Where joys my fellows were?

But joys passed to sorrows as he encountered both physical and spiritual distress, and having had enough he explodes with anger to God:

> Well, I will change the service, and go seek
>   Some other master out.

Prayer as a Place of Transparency

Immediately we see that Herbert experienced prayer as the place of utter transparency before God. In prayer there is no place for false pleasantries, masks, or pretending. In prayer we come before God just as we are, and we lower our self-protective barriers, those shields we put up to protect ourselves from others. As a Christian minister, Herbert comes before God with all his woundedness, fragility, and questions. In his poem "Evensong" Herbert the parson, at the end of a day of ministry, collapses into his stall in the parish church and takes stock of the successes of the day:

> What have I brought thee home
> For this thy love? have I discharged the debt,
>   Which this day's favor did beget?
>   I ran; but all I brought, was foam.
>
>   Thy diet, care, and cost
>   Do end in bubbles, balls of wind;
>   Of wind to thee whom I have crossed,
> But balls of wild-fire to my troubled mind.[12]

Herbert encourages us here to bring to God whatever we face—struggles, burdens or questions—after a day of ministry or giving out. In such metaphors, we can tell God about our struggle for holiness; our perception of failure; a sense of unworthiness; a sense of frustration, in not being effective or successful, not having accomplished what we wanted. We can bring to God a sense of guilt regarding those things "left undone," people unvisited. We can surrender to God our financial worries, health worries, and family concerns. Perhaps we may even join Herbert as he concludes his "Evensong" prayer:

> My God, thou art all love.
>> Not one poor minute escapes thy breast,
>> But brings a favor from above;
> And in this love, more than in bed, I rest.

Prayer as a Place of Transformation

In the poem "The Collar," Herbert suggests that he is like a restless, rebellious, and wayward dog or horse, reluctant to submit himself to the collar or yoke of Christian disciplines ("good cable to enforce and draw"). In it we trace a movement from resistance and protest to ultimate surrender. He begins by expressing a sense of desperation at God:

> I struck the board, and cried, No more;
>> I will abroad.
> What? shall I ever sigh and pine?

After complaining that his only harvest is one of thorns, and his spiritual life is seemingly fruitless, he pauses and catches the echo of God's voice:

> But as I raved and grew more fierce and wild
>> At every word,
> Me thought I heard one calling, *Child;*
>> And I replied, *My Lord.*[13]

Though his spiritual life might be turbulent, underpinning it all is the fundamental, unchangeable reality: he *is* God's child, and he is held in God's love. In "Longing" he comes to see this clearly as the basic truth of his identity. After laying bare his soul's torments, he confesses that to him God is absent, aloof, faraway, and unresponsive:

> With sick and famish'd eyes,
> With doubling knees and weary bones,
>> To thee my cries
>> To thee my groans,
> To thee my sighs, my tears ascend:
>>>> No end?

. . . .
Thou tarriest, while I die,
And fall to nothing: thou dost reign
And rule on high
While I remain
In bitter grief; yet am I styled
Thy child.[14]

Here we see a pilgrimage from despair to a new affirmation and sense of identity as God's beloved one. Herbert teaches us about *movement* in prayer—a movement from questions, burdens, struggles to a place of surrender, an end to resisting, as we "give in" to God. At that point of submission, and at that point alone, we discover God's healing and affirmation. This is explored in the language of Psalms 22 and 42. We see this powerfully expressed in Herbert's poem "Love III." Using the image of God's invitation to the Eucharist, he at first holds back from God through a sense of unworthiness:

Love bade me welcome, yet my soul drew back,
Guilty of dust and sin.

Herbert argues with God and expresses some self-pity, but he finally submits and gives in to God's unconditional grace:

"You must sit down," says Love, "and taste my meat":
So I did sit and eat.[15]

We too can experience transformation, changes in perception, taking place as we pray.

Prayer as a Place of Encounter

Herbert is surprised again and again at the wonder of God's incarnation in Christ, which seems to break into his consciousness at his bleakest moments. In "Redemption" he pictures himself as a tenant seeking to submit a petition to his Lord:

In Heaven at his manor I him sought:
They told me there, that he was lately gone.

So Herbert looks for God among the privileged places of society that he himself had known so well: "in cities, theatres, gardens, parks, and courts." But God is not to be found here.

> At length I heard a ragged noise and mirth
> Of thieves and murderers: there I him espied,
> Who straight, *Your suit is granted* said, and died.[16]

God waits to be discovered in the most unlikely places, among social outcasts and sinners and within the arena of suffering. Christ tells us that he waits to meet us in the hungry, the thirsty, the stranger, the naked, the sick, and even in the imprisoned villain (Matt 25:35-40). All these, he says, are "my brothers and sisters." In this poem, Herbert finds his Lord not in places of security and beauty, but upon a rough-hewn cross. God is not remote from suffering but in the midst of it. As he puts it in "Affliction III":

> My heart did heave, and there came forth,
> *O God!*
> By that I knew that thou wast in the grief,
> To guide and govern it to my relief.

In his powerful composition "The Cross" Herbert comes to realize that the paradoxes of his life are, indeed, cross-shaped. He plays with the metaphor of the cross—he crosses God or finds himself "crossed" or frustrated. Ultimately this leads him to the cross. He reaches the limit of his own strivings:

> And then when after much delay,
> Much wrestling, many a combat, this dear end,
> So much desired, is given, to take away
>   My power to serve thee: to unbend
> All my abilities, my designs confound,
> And lay my threatenings bleeding on the ground.

His angers, his frustrated plans, and the experience of being pulled in different directions all meet in the cross. Indeed, on the cross God has already enfolded and experienced them; he has *felt* them:

> Ah, my dear Father, ease my smart!
> These contrarieties crush me: these cross actions
> Do wear a rope about, and cut my heart:
>   And yet since these thy contradictions
> Are properly a Cross felt by thy Son,
> With but four words, my words, *Thy will be done.*[17]

These insights help us to shape a spirituality of struggle in the face of confusion and even disillusionment. Like some of the psalms, Herbert is able to register a movement in his poems from complaint to acceptance, from rebellion to submission. In his struggles he discovers crucial things *about God and humanity* that cannot be learned from textbooks and sermons, but only from the experience of struggle.

About humanity: that we are called to walk by faith, not by sight (2 Cor 5:7). We are called to tread a path of costly discipleship, not to luxuriate in self-absorption. Jesus calls us to take up our cross daily and follow him (Mark 8:34). We never cease to be loved by God, wanted by God as his child, even when we do not feel his presence. Facts, not feelings, should guide our Christian pilgrimage. When tempted to give up, we should return to the basics, go back to the fundamental reality that no distress can ever fully take away: I am God's child.

About God: Herbert reminds us that God is inscrutable, which means that he is annoying and baffling, as he is beyond the limits of our logic and reason. God constantly surprises us. Everything seems upside down, topsy-turvy in God's ways. He, the mighty one, is to be found precisely in the midst of suffering ones. God himself embraces suffering on the cross and declares himself to be our brother. In prayer, we bring our puzzlement and wonder to God through image and metaphor, and we find our attitudes transformed.

His poem "Priesthood" sums up his discoveries in vivid metaphors. We see ministry, and prayer in particular, as a crucible or furnace where God's Spirit changes our humanity into God-bearing potentiality, as clay is transformed to china by the action of fire.

> Thou art fire, sacred and hallowed fire
> And I but earth and clay.

God longs to form from the clay a beautiful vessel and instrument fit for his use (2 Cor 4:7; 2 Tim 2:20-21).

> God doth often vessels make
> Of lowly matter for high uses meet,
>   I throw me at his feet.

The place where we "throw ourselves at his feet" to be remade and reenergized is the place of prayer.[18]

Questions for Reflection & Discussion

1. What images in this chapter resonate most strongly with your own spiritual journey?

2. What metaphors come to mind for you as you attempt to describe various aspects of the spiritual struggle?

3. What is your experience of "wrestling with God?"

Further Reading

Clements, Arthur L. *Poetry of Contemplation: John Donne, George Herbert, Henry Vaughan and the Modern Period.* New York: State University of New York Press, 1990.

Countryman, L. William. *The Poetic Imagination: An Anglican Spiritual Tradition.* London: Darton, Longman & Todd, 1999.

Hardwick, Peter. "The Inward Struggle of the Self with God: Gerard Manley Hopkins and George Herbert," *The Way* 66 (1989): 6–41.

Herbert, George. *The Works of George Herbert.* Edited by Francis E. Hutchinson. Oxford: Clarendon, 1970.

Sheldrake, Philip. *Love Took My Hand: The Spirituality of George Herbert.* London: Darton, Longman & Todd, 2000.

11

Contemporary Language of Change
and Transformation

> You're my life's adventure;
> Jesus, you're the prize I'm living for.
>
> — Simon Brading and Jules Burt,
> "No One Better"[1]

We explore here contemporary sources that testify to experiences. We will look at three areas where fresh expressions of prayer are evoked: contemporary images in music lyrics, in film, and in technology.

Spirituality of Music

A common theme bubbling up is the movements and transitions in the soul that prove to be life-changing. Our primary source for these testimonies of transformation will be the Kingsway Worship Songbooks popular with young people in charismatic circles.[2] The songs shine with freshness and authenticity; they reveal with clarity the movements of the soul; and they find words and images to communicate and celebrate what God is doing in people's lives. A sense of immediacy and directness reveals itself in the perception of what is happening in people's lives, using metaphors that are mystical, quizzical, raw, and visceral. Five major transitions emerge.

From Fragility to Security

There is a leaving behind of a sense of insecurity and weakness, which involves self-doubt, confusion, meaninglessness, negativity, and fear, together with selfishness and worthlessness. There is a passage toward new confidence, a clear sense of identity in Christ, self-worth, and recognition of potentiality. This involves discovering a purpose to life, a new future, and the experience of being loved and valued by God. Terms are used like "breaking through" and "holding on," both of which testify to regaining focus and fresh empowerment:

> Nothing will change if all the plans I make go wrong,
> Your love stays the same, Your light will guide me through it all.
> I'm hanging on, I'm leaning in to You . . .
> I'm holding on, holding on to You.[3]

From Distance to Embrace

A second experience celebrated in these contemporary songs is the theme of return: a movement away from lostness, alienation, wandering, and distance from God, which involves isolation, loneliness, rootlessness, and disconnection. Something wonderful is discovered: arms of embrace, intimacy, companionship with Jesus, the closeness of the divine presence. Love language is freely used:

> There is no one better,
> There is no one greater;
> Heroes rise but You surpass them all.
> You're my highest pleasure . . .
> I'm running to You.[4]

From Deadness to Reawakening

A third transition is from deadness to awakening the spiritual senses. Part of this experience can be described in terms of a movement from blindness, closed eyes, disorientation toward the opening of spiritual eyes, the ability to see Christ in everyone, new vision, seeing things in full color, new ways of seeing, illumination, enlightenment, wonderment, fresh sense of appreciation, delight in mystery of God's love and self-giving. Cantelon and friends discover a technicolor world of grace:

> Every moment is a movement of grace.
> The world comes alive, You have opened my eyes;
> Everything I see is in color.
> No more black and white..
> The world is alive in You,
> I am alive in You.[5]

From Imprisonment to Liberation

This transition involves a release and rescue from the captivity of guilt, shame, and negativity into unchained liberty and flight. It is a journey from brokenness, fatigue, weariness, and fragmentedness into healing and restoration. Anthony Hoisington and his cowriters want to remind us:

> This is a call to all the dead and disappointed,
> The ones who feel like they are done;
> This is a word to all the ones who feel forgotten,
> But you are not. . .
> We are soaked in all the grace that we've been given,
> Unchained from all that we have done.[6]

Likewise, the Rend Collective Experiment celebrates release:

> You open horizons in my life,
> Of limitless and cloudless hope.
> You defy the gravity in me,
> And give wings to my flightlessness.
> Oh, Christ has set me free
> From negativity, from impossibility . . .
> You have taught my future how to shine,
> All the colors of eternity.
> You've given my soul the space to breathe,
> And discover what it is to simply be.[7]

From Individualism to Community

A fifth movement swings from individualism to a sense of corporate belonging and identity. Sometimes these songs are critiqued because they reveal a low awareness of the need for social justice or wider concern. While songs celebrate God's work in the individual, there emerges a movement from the "I" to the "we":

> You've chased us down with grace,
> You broke through our defence
> We're captured by Your cross . . .
> Where, Lord, could we flee?
> Run a world away, and we could not escape
> Your furious love . . .
> Lord, Your love has no end, it chases us.[8]

Kathryn Scott testifies:

> From the thankful heart to the battle scarred,
> From the comforted to those who grieve,
> From the mountain top to the empty cup,
> From the waiting to those who have received,
> We cry out as one:
> We still believe . . .
>
> From the reborn hope to the weary soul,
> From the quest for truth to those who see,
> From the soaring wings to the shattered dream,
> From the broken to those who have been healed,
> We cry out as one:
> Through the fire, through the pain,
> We offer You our "yes" again.[9]

A corporate vocation becomes crystallized and clarified:

> We will be a church that stands for justice . . .
> We will be a church that's breaking through
> We will be a church that shakes religion,
> We will be a church that's free of condemnation
> We will be a church that impacts the nation . . .
> We will be a church that makes a difference.[10]

Spirituality of Film

Movies furnish us with a rich vocabulary with which to describe the spiritual life. Unfolding narratives resonate with parts of our experience, while the choices and dilemmas of characters reverberate with our own struggles. Sometimes this opens up a fresh perspective or helps us to clarify the issues and questions that we face. Here we offer some examples.

The theme of vocation and potentiality is explored in the British film *Billy Elliot*, which explores the issues of self-worth and acceptance. Big choices emerge in *Schindler's List*. We encounter a treatment of discernment in *The Lord of the Rings* trilogy. Issues of forgiveness are raised by *Dead Man Walking*, while *The Shawshank Redemption* invites us to reconsider the nature of hope. The nature of prayer emerges in *Shadowlands* while *The City of God* challenges our response to poverty and social injustice. *Amadeus* asks us to consider how God gives extraordinary abilities to people, like Mozart, who might be considered by some undeserving or unworthy. *Samsara* looks at disparate and contradictory human activities across the world, with juxtapositions that challenge us to the core. *Inception* asks about states of wakefulness and the origins of ideas, while *The Matrix* gives us another take on what is real and what is not. *Blade Runner* questions what it is to be mortal and confronts us with questions about human imperfections.[11]

Many cinematic metaphors in film scenes are archetypal in nature, echoing what we have encountered thus far:

- weather: fierce lightening may foreshadow unexpected changes; floods evoke threat and danger;
- sounds: waves crashing on rocks suggest emotional turmoil;
- colors: black, grey, white, red, and green each designate an emotion or state;
- birds: black crows express fear or threat; signets and swans anticipate growth and freedom;
- animals: foxes, snakes, spiders each carry their own symbolic meanings;
- plants: herbs, sunflowers evoke healing and hopefulness;
- the advent of light and dark, dawn and dusk all suggest shifting human emotions;
- actions: dancing, violence, theft, journey, and eating each carry symbolic meanings.

Such a diverse range of metaphors invite us indeed to seek God in all things, and recognize the sacramentality of daily life.

Spirituality of the Internet

Today's world—dominated as it is by information technology and digital gadgetry—suggests many images and metaphors that can be used in spiritual conversations. Language is making a transition—icons and fonts are not what they used to be! The Internet search engine becomes a symbol of humanity's quest for answers, and a preoccupation with "surfing the net" reveals the restlessness of the human heart. "Googling" is a contemporary preoccupation. We note five transitions in the recent use of language.

Identity: From Authenticity to Artificiality

The development of computers mirrors the human soul. In the past we spoke of being made in God's image—today we realize that we are "hard-wired" for God. Moore and Gillette comment that archetypes are the "hard-wired components of our genetically transmitted psychic machine."[12] The hard drive of our being is designed for communication with God; this is a basic fact of our human "operating system."

As we explored in our opening chapter, our basic identity is rooted in a realization that each person is a child of God, uniquely gifted and cherished by God. But modern technology can not only depersonalize us so we become anonymous consumers, it can also lead to a dichotomy between "online" and "offline" personalities. We can create "digital alter egos" as websites urge us to "create a platform." We can choose our own "avatar" symbol to represent us in a chat room. Identities can be falsified. There are massive dangers of superficiality and deception in Internet use, and people can end up living in a virtual world divorced from reality. Encryption and decoding may speak of the need for secrecy or represent a cover-up. Pseudonyms and nicknames may represent a need to conceal through gender or age. In the passion for taking "selfies" one can choose the background and those to be pictured with, altering details at will. The spiritual autobiography of the past has given way to Facebook pages and one's (edited) personal profile. "Private" browsing can either safeguard a sense of personal respect or provide a cloak for mischief![13]

All this has tremendous potential for helping us explore real issues in spiritual direction. The basic question remains: Who am I? How can I be my true, authentic self? Is there any place for wearing different personas or masks with God? Since Adam, we have been tempted to hide from God, but as David came to realize in his penitential psalm:

> You desire truth in the inward being;
> therefore teach me wisdom in my secret heart. (Ps 51:6)

Belonging: From Communion to Connectivity

One priority of our times is the constant desire to be connected to the Internet and to reach out across cyberspace. If we are not able to be connected, we cannot take part in any form of electronic communication. Having a Wi-Fi connection is key. We must get "online"—plug in, switch on, and log in. Spirits sink when we get the message "Your browser is not responding." We hate it when the system crashes, the computer runs slow, or the mobile phone signal breaks up. We need to be properly tuned and have our personal settings just right or things won't work. Useful and resonant metaphors emerge here. Connectivity is the basic essential. Using a mobile phone reminds us that God can call at any time or place, but we can be switched off or be in "sleep" mode! A minister said to me recently about listening to God: "Prayer is about tuning into God's wavelength, not making a broadcast from one's own station."

In the past we spoke of our relationships with God and one another in terms of spiritual communion within the mystical body of Christ. Today we have a different way of relating as we participate in a social networking world. We are urged to get "linked-in." We belong to a "virtual community"—we may have many contacts called "friends" but such so-called friendship may be a mile wide and an inch deep. This prompts various challenging questions in spiritual direction.

Communicating: From Listening to God to Instant Messaging

The acquisition of information or data is one of today's imperatives. While the Book of Common Prayer speaks of "hearing and receiving God's holy Word," this priority may today be translated into the language of downloading God's Word into our hearts. Today as we download apps, articles, movies, music, and YouTube clips, we remind ourselves that we actually need to do something about the download—otherwise it simply clutters the space in our memory devices.

Communication lies at the heart of the culture of the Internet. Where in the past we offered "arrow prayers" like "O God make haste to help me!" (Ps 38:22), today people talk of instant messaging and tweeting God. There is a need for immediate gratification or response; we do not like to wait. Speed matters. Pressure on time is an issue—one priest said to me recently, "I text God, not write a letter." "Tweets" to God may convey the sense that God is available and interested in our goings-on, or they may trivialize our life so that we miss the bigger spiritual issues. Referring to an online video call, a recent spiritual writer asks: "Is it fanciful to see the electronic realm which brought our son almost literally before us as an analogy of the spiritual realm through which God brings himself before us? Could we say that prayer is akin to Skyping?"[14]

Reflecting: From Journaling to Blogging

Individualism and self-preoccupation within a narcissistic postmodern culture reveals itself in the need some have to "blog," replacing the slower reflective handwritten journaling of old. There is a shift from reference to "affections" to the declaration of feelings; a movement from facts to experience, from "the" story to "my" story; and emoticons can be inserted into messages to symbolize current states of mind.

Expressing: From Sin and Worship to Virus and Awe

Today people express a worshipful or reverent attitude when they express their gratefulness for inventiveness, and appreciation of contemporary design, ergonomics, and technological breakthroughs. Words like "cool," "magic," and "wicked" form a part of our daily vocabulary. There has been the rediscovery of the use of the word "awesome."

Outmoded and unpopular concepts like "sin" might be conveyed through the imagery of being infected with a virus, cyber-attacks, things going viral. There is a diversity of images and metaphors that can be used in spiritual direction and in communicating the faith.

There is the risk of consumerist detachment replacing real engagement. There is much talk—and less walk: too much information, too little formation. The imperative is to connect with the culture and notice images that might illuminate our understanding of the spiritual life and equip us for its expression. Looking at our hymnbooks or songbooks, we might note a transition in metaphors from the sixties to the present:

> God of concrete, God of steel,
> God of piston and of wheel,
> God of pylon, God of steam,
> God of girder and of beam,
> God of atom, God of mine,
> All the world of power is thine! (1969)[15]

> My concrete heart won't stop me . . .
> I'll sing like it's the first time
> And leave behind the cynic in my soul
> We're letting praise like fireworks
> Loose from our thankful hearts. (2012)[16]

A Choice of Operating Systems

One recent spiritual writer utilizes the imagery of the computer operating system. Cynthia Bourgeault suggests that we have a default operating system: "The system already installed in us is a binary operating system. It runs on the power of 'either/or.' . . . The egoic operating system is really a grammar of perception, a way of making sense of the world by dividing the field into subject and object, inside and outside." Bourgeault tells us that we construct our sense of identity through such a dualistic mind-set of "us and them" and we differentiate ourselves from others by highlighting what separates us off. But Jesus offers us an alternative:

This other operating system (we can call it the nondual system or the unitive sytem, if we want) is the operating system of the heart. . . . a different way of perceiving. Rather than dividing and conquering, it connects with a seamless and indivisible reality through a whole different way of organizing the informational field. . . . Jesus' whole mission can fundamentally be seen as trying to push, tease, shock, and wheedle people beyond the "limited analytic intellect" of their egoic operating system into the "vast realm of the mind" where they will discover the resources they need to live in fearlessness, coherence, and compassion—or in other words, as true human beings.[17]

She finds in this computer metaphor a powerful image with which to approach the alternative liberating wisdom of Jesus.

Into the Cloud

One feature of current technology is the importance of the "cloud." It has come to represent the area in cyberspace where data can be stored and from which resources may be accessed by the user. Internet companies now also talk of the "cloud meeting," where people meet in video conferencing, online gatherings, and share group chat. The information cloud has become the cloud of meeting, a "place" of encounter. In our next chapter we will see how this takes us right back to Mount Sinai and a "cloud of unknowing"!

Questions for Reflection and Discussion

1. Which images from the present culture resonate most strongly with your spiritual journey?

2. How would you explain the Christian faith in a way that avoids theological jargon and utilizes contemporary imagery?

3. Which of the computer images strikes you the most? Why?

Further Reading

Hollingshurst, Steve. *Mission-Shaped Evangelism: The Gospel in Contemporary Culture.* Norwich: Canterbury, 2010.

Lakoff, George. *Metaphors We Live By.* Chicago: University of Chicago Press, 2003.

12

Language of Darkness and Cloud:
Beyond Words and Images

Syllabled by silence, let me hear
The still small voice which reached
the prophet's ear

—John Greenleaf Whittier [1]

"There is a time to speak, and a time to keep silence" (Eccl 3:7). We conclude our explorations of spiritual vocabulary by attending to four spiritual writers who have an important message for us, summarized in the words: "O do shut up!" Certainly, the cataphatic tradition, the *via positiva*, which delights in vivid metaphors and images, must be complemented by the apophatic way, the *via negativa*, which tells us that we need to go beyond images, as they are only a starting point. As Meister Eckhart affirms: "The freer you are from images the more receptive you are to his interior operation." [2]

Gregory of Nyssa was the first writer to develop this message through the image of darkness; it was to become an important strand in thinking of spiritual development throughout the history of Christian spirituality. Jean Danielou puts it: "In Gregory of Nyssa . . . the term 'darkness' takes on a new meaning and an essentially mystical connotation. . . . Gregory's originality consists in the fact that he was the first to express this characteristic of the highest stages of mystical experience." [3] His *Life of Moses*, a map of the Christian pilgrimage as it is suggested to him by the Exodus accounts, culminates in the ascent of the mountain of divine knowledge, represented in Sinai. Gregory claims that an integral element in the Christian pilgrimage is the encounter with divine darkness:

> For leaving behind everything that is observed, not only what sense comprehends but also what the intelligence thinks it sees, it keeps

on penetrating deeper until by the intelligence's yearning for understanding it gains access to the invisible and the incomprehensible, and
there it sees God. This is the true knowledge of what is sought; this
is the seeing that consists in not seeing, because that which is sought
transcends all knowledge, being separated on all sides by incompre-
hensibility as by a kind of darkness. Wherefore John the sublime,
who penetrated into the luminous darkness, says, "No one has ever
seen God," thus asserting that knowledge of the divine essence is
unattainable not only by men but also by every intelligent creature.

When, therefore, Moses grew in knowledge, he declared that he
had seen God in the darkness, that is, that he had then come to know
that what is divine is beyond all knowledge and comprehension, for
the text says, "Moses approached the dark cloud where God was."
What God? He who "made darkness his hiding place," as David says,
who also was initiated into the mysteries in the same inner sanctuary.[4]

In Moses' first encounter with God in the burning bush, God appears
as light, as illumination. For Gregory this represents the beginning of the
Christian conversion, a turning from the darkness of falsehood to the light
of Christ. This process of illumination, for beginners, involves a purification of the soul from foreign elements. However, as the Christian, like
Moses, progresses along the spiritual journey, he or she is led into darkness—not a negative darkness but a "luminous darkness." This represents
the unknowability of God: this is the apophatic spiritual path, which falls
silent before the unspeakable mystery of God. As Danielou puts it:

After learning all that can be known of God, the soul discovers the
limits of this knowledge; and this discovery is an advance, because
now there is an awareness of the divine transcendence and incompre-
hensibility. We have then arrived at a negative, "apophatic" theology.
For we have now an authentic experience, a true vision. And the
darkness is a positive reality that helps us to know God—that is why
it is called luminous. For it implies an awareness of God that transcends all determination, and thus it is far truer than any determined
categorical knowledge. For here in this obscurity the soul experiences
the transcendence of the divine nature, that infinite distance by which
God surpasses all creation.[5]

Andrew Louth explains: "It is an experience beyond the senses and
beyond the intellect; it is a feeling awareness of a fragrance that delights
and enraptures the soul."[6] In the fifth century, the writer known as Dionysius develops the thought of Gregory:

Trinity!! Higher than any being,
  any divinity, any goodness!
Guide of Christians
  in the wisdom of heaven!
Lead us up beyond unknowing and light,
  up to the farthest, highest peak
    of mystic scripture,
  where the mysteries of God's Word
    lie simple, absolute and unchangeable
    in the brilliant darkness of a hidden silence.
Amid the deepest shadow
  they pour overwhelming light
  on what is most manifest.
Amid the wholly unsensed and unseen
  they completely fill our sightless minds
  with treasures beyond all beauty.[7]

Dionysius echoes the thought of Gregory of Nyssa; indeed, he seems to have known his *Life of Moses*, as he too uses a similar image to explore the significance of darkness. Thus he writes:

Leave behind you everything perceived and understood, everything perceptible and understandable, all that is not and all that is, and, with your understanding laid aside, strive upward as much as you can toward union with him who is beyond all being and knowledge. By an undivided and absolute abandonment of yourself and everything, shedding all and freed from all, you will be uplifted to the ray of the divine shadow which is above everything that is.[8]

Within his Christianized Neo-Platonism, Dionysius finds the apex of the spiritual search.[9] Later, two major writers develop Dionysius' thinking. They both call us to silence our word-filled prayers and leave behind the complex of images and metaphors. Saint John of the Cross summons us into the dark night:

O guiding night!
O night more lovely than the dawn!
O night that has united
the Lover with his beloved,
  transforming the beloved in her Lover!

This sixteenth-century Spanish mystic gave three reasons for using this image to describe aspects of the spiritual journey:

> We can offer three reasons for calling this journey toward union
> with God a night. The first has to do with the point of departure,
> because individuals must deprive themselves of their appetites for
> worldly possessions. This denial and privation is like a night for all
> one's senses. The second reason refers to the means or the road along
> which a person travels to this union. Now this road is faith, and for
> the intellect faith is also like a dark night. The third reason pertains
> to the point of arrival, namely God. And God is also a dark night to
> the soul in this life. . . These nights pass through a soul, or better,
> the soul passes through them in order to reach union with God.[10]

First, says John, in the dark we cannot actually see. In the deeper
reaches of prayer, the Christian needs to shut down his or her five senses
because they hold one captive in a state of attachment to the material
world and activate one's self-seeking appetites.

Second, in the dark one cannot easily make out obstacles or turnings
along the path, so one must move forward in trust. "We walk by faith,
not by sight." In one's relationship with God, John teaches, one must take
the risk of moving forward without knowing the precise route, venturing
into the unknown, where visibility is nil.

Third, John says, the darkness speaks of God himself as mystery. God
is not something one can box in and neatly label—God is quite beyond
humanity's best concepts and categories. But "the dark night of the soul" is
not for John a negative experience; it is, rather, a time of growth and healing. The night, for John, is a place of radical transformation. It represents
a time when one allows God to do his work powerfully within, reshaping
and redirecting the ego, and leading one into a greater surrender to him.
Writing on John of the Cross in his classic book *The Wound of Knowledge*,
Rowan Williams reminds us:

> Illumination is the running-out of language and thought, the compul-
> sion exercised by a reality drastically and totally beyond the reach of
> our conceptual apparatus. . . . Real knowledge of God cannot be put
> into words with any approximation to completeness; thus real and
> personal knowledge of God cannot be identified with words in the
> understanding. . . . God himself breaks and reshapes all religious
> language as he acts through vulnerability, failure and contradiction.[11]

The fourteenth-century text *The Cloud of Unknowing* provides us,
on the one hand, with a vocabulary with which to articulate the inner
stirrings of prayer, while on the other hand it calls us to wordless silence.
It offers a framework of beliefs as a tool with which the reader can begin

to name and make sense of subjective experience. *The Cloud* works with a psychology of the time with its theory about the faculties of the soul (chaps 62–66). It highlights the importance of the will in responding to God, and downplays the role of imagination and what it calls "sensuality." But it allows for the affective aspects of prayer, rather than the cognitive aspects. *The Cloud* can say of God: "He may well be loved, but not thought. By love he can be caught and held, but by thinking never."[12]

The author of *The Cloud* teaches that there are various signs, clues, or evidences that suggest that the reader may be ready to make a transition in their praying from discursive, active thinking with words and images, as in meditations on the passion, toward the wordless silence and solitude of contemplation. One key indicator is that of desire or yearning: "It seems to me, in my rough and ready way, that there are four states or kinds of Christian life, and they are these: Common, Special, Solitary, and Perfect. . . . I think that our Lord in his great mercy has called you in the same order and in the same way, leading you on to himself by your heart-felt desire."[13]

The Cloud offers guidelines for the task of discernment, to be worked through with a "discreet director." Sometimes it will be necessary to exercise extreme caution in interpreting unbidden feelings: "All other comforts, sounds, gladness, sweetness that come suddenly to you from outside, please do suspect! They can be good or evil; the work of a good angel if good, and of an evil angel if evil."[14] And so the author aims to be as directive and clear as possible: "So when you feel by the grace of God that he is calling you to this work, and you intend to respond, lift up your heart to God with humble love. . . . It all depends on your desire."[15] But there are reasons for caution: "So for the love of God be careful in this matter, and do not overstrain yourself emotionally or beyond your strength. . . . [Such strainings] sorely hurt the silly soul, and it festers in feigned and fiendish fantasies! So beware of behaving wildly like some animal, and learn to love God with quiet, eager joy, at rest in body as in soul."[16]

The wisdom contained in *The Cloud* resonates strongly with the story of the transfiguration. On Mount Tabor, Peter's instinct is to construct tents, domesticate the divine, contain the mystery, and regain control in the situation: "Let us build three booths" (Luke 9:33). This can represent our attempts in prayer to "get a handle" on God, to box him in with words, concepts, and images, and to encase divinity with human structures. But precisely at the point when Peter suggests the building of booths, "a cloud came and overshadowed them; and they were afraid as they entered the cloud" (Luke 9:34). The response to human tent-building is a divine drenching in mysterious wet mist where visibility is reduced to nil. The cloud now dampens the senses and exuberant conceptualizing and silences the overactive mind. The cloud eclipses the sun: there has been a change in the weather from bright sunlight to darkening cloud, gloom, and impenetrable haze. A swirling fog blankets the disciples. In the cloud one feels out of control, not knowing which way to turn. It turns out to be a poignant symbol of that transition in prayer from active, discursive thinking to simpler loving. As the author of *The Cloud* puts it, calling us to apophatic prayer, the *via negativa*, while cautious about the use of vivid images in relation to speaking of God:

> When you first begin, you find only darkness and as it were a cloud of unknowing. You don't know what this means except that in your will you feel a simple steadfast intention reaching out towards God. . . . Reconcile yourself to wait in this darkness as long as is necessary, but still go on longing after him whom you love. For if you are to feel him or to see him in this life, it must always be in this cloud, in this darkness.[17]

This metaphor instructs the present writer to lay down his pen, to cease explorations of words, pictures, and metaphors, and to come before God in silent, awe-filled wonder. As Bernard of Clairvaux put it in the great hymn *Jesu, dulcis memoria*:

> Jesus the very thought of thee
> With sweetness fills the breast. . . .
> To those who ask how kind thou art,
> How good to those who seek! . . .
> But what to those who find? Ah, this
> Nor tongue nor pen can show.[18]

Questions for Reflection and Discussion

1. What signs, clues, or evidences do you sense—in yourself, or in the person you are accompanying—that it is time to inch forward into a type of prayer that is more contemplative and silent?

2. How do you find silent prayer, a prayer beyond images? Is it something you welcome or fear? Why?

3. How would you go about encouraging another person to leave behind words and images in active-brained meditation and enter a more receptive, wondering, mystical type of prayer?

4. What discoveries of God have you made in silent prayer? What have you found out about yourself?

Further Reading

Lyddon, Eileen, *Door Through Darkness: St. John of the Cross and Mysticism in Everyday Life.* London: New City, 1994.

Turner, Denys. *The Darkness of God: Negativity in Christian Mysticism.* Cambridge: Cambridge University Press, 1995.

Notes

Preface—(pages vii–xi)

1. Francis Thompson, "In No Strange Land," *Complete Poetical Works* (London: Brooks, 2007), 356.

2. William A. Barry and William J. Connolly, *The Practice of Spiritual Direction* (New York: Seabury, 1982), 67.

3. Francisco de Osuna, *The Third Spiritual Alphabet*, trans. Mary E. Giles, Classics of Western Spirituality (New York: Paulist, 1981), 39.

4. Ibid., 7.

5. Micheal O'Siadhail, *Tongues* (Tarset, Northumberland: Bloodaxe, 2010), 11.

6. Philip Sheldrake, *Spirituality & History: Questions of Interpretation and Method* (London: SPCK, 1991), 165.

7. Carolyn Gratton, *The Art of Spiritual Guidance* (New York: Crossroad, 1992), 31.

8. Joseph Campbell, *Thou Art That: Transforming Religious Metaphor* (Novato, CA: New World Library, 2013), 6.

9. Sandra M. Schneiders, "Approaches to the Study of Christian Spirituality," in *The Blackwell Companion to Christian Spirituality*, ed. Arthur Holder (Oxford: Wiley-Blackwell, 2005), 15–34.

10. John Hick, *The Metaphor of God Incarnate: Christology in a Pluralistic Age* (London: SCM, 1993), 100.

11. Margaret Guenther, *Holy Listening: The Art of Spiritual Direction* (Lanham, MD: Rowman & Littlefield, 1992).

12. Kathleen Fischer, *Women at the Well: Feminist Perspectives on Spiritual Direction* (London: SPCK, 1988), 65–66.

1 Mystic Metaphors—(pages 1–8)

1. Joseph Campbell, *Thou Art That: Transforming Religious Metaphor* (Novato, CA: New World Library, 2013), 9 .

2. Jürgen Moltmann, *The Spirit of Life: A Universal Affirmation* (Minneapolis: Fortress, 2001), 285.

3. Sue Pickering, *Spiritual Direction: A Practical Introduction* (Norwich: Canterbury, 2008), 104–5.

4. Janet K. Ruffing, *To Tell the Sacred Tale: Spiritual Direction and Narrative* (Mahwah, NJ: Paulist, 2011), 90, 91.

5. Paul Avis, *God and the Creative Imagination: Metaphor, Symbol and Myth in Religion and Theology* (London: Routledge, 1999), 102. See also Paul Ricoeur, *The Rule of Metaphor: Multi-disciplinary Studies of the Creation of Meaning in Language*, University of Toronto Romance Series (Toronto: University of Toronto Press, 1978); David E. Cooper, *Metaphor*, Aristotelian Society Series (Oxford: Blackwell, 1986); Hick, *The Metaphor of God Incarnate*; Lynn Fainsilber, and Andrew Ortony, "Metaphorical Uses of Language in the Expression of Emotions," *Metaphor and Symbolic Activity* 2, no. 4 (1987): 239–50.

6. Avis, *Creative Imagination*, 97.

7. Brian Wren, *What Language Shall I Borrow? God-Talk in Worship* (London: SCM, 1989), 92.

8. Sallie McFague, *Metaphorical Theology: Models of God in Religious Language* (Philadelphia: Fortress, 1982).

9. Walter Brueggemann, *The Prophetic Imagination* (Minneapolis: Fortress, 2001).

10. Rowan Williams, *The Edge of Words: God and the Habits of Language* (London: Bloomsbury, 2014), 130.

11. Richard Harries, "God talk and normal talk," *Church Times*, October 24, 2014.

12. Colin E. Gunton, *The Actuality of Atonement: A Study of Metaphor, Rationality and the Christian Tradition* (Edinburgh: T & T Clark, 1988), 51.

13. L. William Countryman, *The Poetic Imagination: An Anglican Spiritual Tradition* (London: Darton, Longman & Todd, 1999), 28.

14. John Macquarrie, *Thinking about God* (New York: Harper & Row, 1975), 13.

15. Stanley J. Grenz, *A Primer on Postmodernism* (Grand Rapids, MI: William B. Eerdmans, 1996).

16. David Tracy, *The Analogical Imagination: Christian Theology and the Culture of Pluralism* (New York: Crossroad, 1981), 407.

17. Janet Martin Soskice, *Metaphor and Religious Language* (Oxford: Clarendon Press, 1985), 31. See also George Lakoff and Mark Johnson, *Metaphors We Live By* (Chicago: University of Chicago Press, 1980).

18. George Herbert, "Prayer (I)" *The Temple* (Cambridge, 1633); Rowan Williams, *Teresa of Avila* (London: Continuum, 1991), 156.

19. Fraser Watts and Mark Williams, *The Psychology of Religious Knowing* (London: Chapman, 1988), 115.

20. Ibid., 113.

21. Laurence B. Brown, *The Human Side of Prayer: The Psychology of Praying* (Birmingham, AL: Religious Education, 1994), 63.

22. Ann and Barry Ulanov, *Primary Speech: A Psychology of Prayer* (Atlanta: John Knox Press, 1982), 2.

23. Ibid, 122. Compare arguments of experiences of God as perception in William P. Alston, *Perceiving God: The Epistemology of Religious Experience* (Ithaca, NY: Cornell University Press, 1991).

24. Tjeu van Knippenberg, "The Structure and Variety of Prayer," *Journal of Empirical Theology* 13, no. 2 (2000): 55-67.

25. Watts and Williams, recognizing the difficulty of individuals articulating "raw insights" gained in prayer, note that a process similar to that in psychotherapy is needed: a movement towards 'symbolization' or 'articulate conceptualization.' Watts and Williams, *The Psychology of Religious Knowing*, 72.

26. Joseph Campbell, in a workshop on "The Mystery and the Essence of Life," qtd. by Arlene F. Harder, "An Agnostic's Encounter with God," www .support4change.com.

27. Caroline Franks Davis, *The Evidential Force of Religious Experience* (Oxford: Clarendon Press, 1989), 147.

28. Nevertheless, she is emphatic: "The fact that an experience has been 'interpreted' in terms of a specific conceptual framework or mental model (religious or otherwise) cannot in itself make that experience evidentially suspect." Ibid., 148.

29. Soskice, *Metaphor and Religious Language*, 160.

30. *Funeral Services of the Christian Churches in England* (Norwich: Canterbury, 2001).

31. *The Roman Missal, Third Typical Edition* (Washington, DC: International Commission on English in the Liturgy, 2010).

32. Jean Maalouf, *Jesus Laughed and Other Reflections on Being Human* (Kansas City, MO: Sheed & Ward, 1996), 73.

2 The Tender and Risky Language of Children, Friends, Lovers—
(pages 9–21)

1. Eugene H. Peterson, *The Contemplative Pastor: Returning to the Art of Spiritual Direction* (Grand Rapids, MI: William B. Eerdmans, 1989).

2. Bruce J. Malina, *The New Testament World: Insights from Cultural Anthropology* (Louisville, KY: John Knox Press, 2001).

3. Julian of Norwich, *Showings*, trans. Edmund Colledge and James Walsh, Classics of Western Spirituality (New York: Paulist, 1978), 183.

4. Ibid., 299–300.

5. Henri. J. M. Nouwen, *Intimacy: Pastoral Psychology Essays* (San Francisco: Harper & Row, 1969), 52.

6. Kathleen Fischer, *Women at the Well*, 53, 55.

7. Richard Rohr, *From Wild Man to Wise Man: Reflections on Male Spirituality* (Cincinnati, OH: St. Anthony Messenger, 2005). See also David C. James, *What Are They Saying about Masculine Spirituality?* (Mahwah, NJ: Paulist, 1996).

8. Archbishops' Council, *Common Worship: Daily Prayer* (London: Church House, 2011).

9. Aelred of Rievaulx, "Spiritual Friendship," in *The Cistercian World: Monastic Writings of the Twelfth Century*, trans. Pauline Matarasso (London: Penguin, 1993), 179, 190.

10. Ibid, 185.

11. Marilyn Sewell, introduction to *Cries of the Spirit: A Celebration of Women's Spirituality*, ed. Marilyn Sewell (Boston: Beacon, 1991), 3. See also Philip Sheldrake, *Befriending our Desires* (London: Darton, Longman & Todd, 2012).

12. *From Glory to Glory: Texts from Gregory of Nyssa's Mystical Writings*, trans. Herbert Musurillo (New York: St. Vladimir's Seminary Press, 2001).

13. *The Song of Songs: Selections from the Sermons of St Bernard of Clairvaux*, ed. Halcyon Backhouse (London: Hodder & Stoughton, 1990), 38.

14. Richard of St. Victor, "The Four Degrees of Violent Charity," in *On Love*, trans. Hugh Feiss, Victorine Texts in Translation 2 (Hyde Park, NY: New City Press, 2012).

15. *Meditations with Meister Eckhart*, trans. Matthew Fox (Rochester, VT: Bear, 1983), 88, 81.

16. *Hadewijch: The Complete Works*, trans. Columbo Hart, Classics of Western Spirituality (Mahwah, NJ: Paulist, 1980), 165. See also Grace M. Jantzen, *Power, Gender and Christian Mysticism*, Cambridge Studies in Ideology and Religion (Cambridge: Cambridge University Press, 1995), 134–46, and John Giles Milhaven, *Hadewijch and Her Sisters: Other Ways of Loving and Knowing*, The Body in Culture, History, and Religion (Albany, NY: State University of New York Press, 1993).

17. Caroline Walker Bynum, *Jesus as Mother: Studies in the Spirituality of the High Middle Ages* (Berkeley, CA: University of California Press, 1982), 202.

18. *The Collected Works of St. John of the Cross*, trans. Kieran Kavanaugh & Otilio Rodriguez (Washington, DC: Institute of Carmelite Studies, 1991), 475.

19. See, for example, Dianne Bergant, *Song of Songs: The Love Poetry of Scripture* (Hyde Park, NY: New City Press, 1998); Janet K. Ruffing, *Spiritual Direction: Beyond the Beginnings* (Mahwah, NJ: Paulist, 2000), 95–124.

20. Thomas Traherne, *Centuries* (London: Faith, 1960), 112.

21. *The Love Poems of Rumi*, ed. Deepak Chopra (New York: Harmony, 1998).

22. For the former, see Leon J. Podles, *The Church Impotent: The Feminization of Christianity* (Dallas, TX: Spence, 1999); for the latter, see Nicola Slee, *Praying Like a Woman* (London: SPCK, 2004), and Rohr, *From Wild Man to Wise Man*.

23. Richard Rohr, *Unitive Consciousness: Beyond Gender* (Albuquerque, NM: Center for Action & Contemplation, 2012), 1.

3 The Inspirational Language of Poets and Artists—(pages 22–34)

1. "God's Grandeur," in *Gerald Manley Hopkins: The Major Works*, ed. C. Phillips (Oxford: Oxford University Press, 1986), 128.

2. William Blake, "Auguries of Innocence," *The Complete Poetry and Prose of William Blake*, ed. David V. Erdman (New York: Anchor, 1997), 490.

3. See, for example, Joseph M. Stoutzenberger and John D. Bohrer, *Praying with Francis of Assisi* (Winona, MN: Saint Mary's Press, 1989).

4. For a recent exploration of garden imagery see Jennifer Rees Larcombe, *A Year's Journey with God* (London: Hodder & Stoughton, 2013).

5. Peter Dronke, in *Hildegard of Bingen: An Anthology*, ed. Fiona Bowie and Oliver Davies (London: SPCK, 1990), 32.

6. Ibid., 32.

7. Evelyn Underhill, "Planting-time," in *Immanence: A Book of Verses* (London: J. M. Dent & Sons, 1915).

8. J. M. C. Crum, "Now the Green Blade Riseth from the Buried Grain," *Oxford Book of Carols* (Oxford: Oxford University Press, 1928).

9. R. S. Thomas, *Laboratories of the Spirit* (London: Macmillan, 1975), poem called "The Flower."

10. D. H. Lawrence, "Shadows," *Complete Poems*, Penguin Classics (London: Penguin, 1994).

11. Gerard Manley Hopkins, "Thou art indeed just, Lord, if I content," *Poems and Prose*, Penguin Classics (London: Penguin, 1985).

12. John of Damascus, "Ode 1," in *Hymns of the Eastern Church*, trans. J. M. Neale (London: J. T. Hayes, 1862), 53–54.

13. William Blake, "The Tyger," in *The Complete Poetry & Prose of William Blake*, edited by David V. Erdman (New York: Anchor, 1988), 24.

14. Vladimir Lossky, *The Mystical Theology of the Eastern Church* (London: James Clarke, 1957), 223 .

15. Symeon the New Theologian, "You O Christ are the Kingdom of Heaven," *Divine Eros: Hymns of St. Symeon the New Theologian*, trans. Daniel K. Griggs, Popular Patristics Series 40 (Yonkers, NY: St. Vladimir's Seminary Press, 2011). See also John W. Oliver, *Giver of Life: The Holy Spirit in Orthodox Tradition* (Brewster, MA: Paraclete, 2011) and George A. Maloney, *The Mystic of Fire and Light: St. Symeon the New Theologian* (Denville, NJ: Dimension, 1975).

16. See, for example, Maria Beesing, Robert J. Nogosek, and Patrick H. O'Leary, *The Enneagram: A Journey of Self Discovery* (Denville, New Jersey: Dimension Books, 1984).

17. *Francis de Sales: Introduction to the Devout Life*, trans. Michael Day (Wheathampstead: Anthony Clarke, 1962), 11, 159.

18. Nick Holtam, *The Art of Worship: Paintings, Prayers and Readings for Meditation* (London: National Gallery, 2011), 3.

19. Sybil MacBeth, *Praying in Color: Drawing a New Path to God* (Brewster, MA: Paraclete, 2007). Julia Cameron, *The Artist's Way: A Course in Discovering and Recovering Your Creative Self* (London: Pan, 1995). Christopher Irvine, *The Art of God: The Making of Christians and the Meaning of Worship* (London: SPCK, 2005).

20. Qtd. in Cynthia Freeland, *Art Theory: A Very Short Introduction* (Oxford: Oxford University Press, 2001), 104.

21. Herbert Read, *The Meaning of Art* (London: Faber & Faber, 1931), 39.

22. Gabriele Finaldi, *The Image of Christ: The Catalogue of the Exhibition "Seeing Salvation"* (London: National Gallery, 2000).

23. Bruce Duncan, *Pray Your Way: Your Personality and God* (London: Darton, Longman & Todd, 1993).

4 The Invigorating Language of Singers and Dancers—(pages 35–45)

1. Gen 1; Rev 5:9-10; 7:15-17; 11:17-18; 15:3-4; 19:6-9.

2. Raymond E. Brown, *The Birth of the Messiah: A Commentary on the Infancy Narratives in the Gospels of Matthew and Luke* (New York: Doubleday, 1977).

3. See Rev 4:10-11; 5:8-10; 7:9-12; 11:16-18; 12:7-12; 15:2-4; 19:1-5.

4. Rosalind Brown, *How Hymns Shape our Lives*, Grove Spirituality Series (Cambridge: Grove, 2001).

5. Ann and Barry Ulanov, *Primary Speech: A Psychology of Prayer* (Atlanta: John Knox Press, 1982).

6. Sydney Carter, "Lord of the Dance" (London: Stainer & Bell, 1963). Used with permission.

7. John Gardner, *Tomorrow Shall Be My Dancing Day* (Oxford: Oxford University Press, 1966).

8. Qtd. in *The Gnostic Bible*, ed. Willis Barnstone and Marvin Meyer (Boston: Shambhala, 2006), 352.

9. Thomas Merton, *Seeds of Contemplation* (Wheathampstead: Anthony Clarke, 1961), 230.

10. C. Baxter Kruger, *The Great Dance: The Christian Vision Revisited* (Vancouver, BC: Regent College, 2005), 87.

11. Ibid., 18.

12. Elizabeth Johnson, qtd. in Robin Greenwood, *Transforming Church: Liberating Structures for Ministry* (London: SPCK, 2002), 67.

13. Leonardo Boff, *Trinity and Society* (Maryknoll, NY: Orbis, 1988), 6.

14. C. S. Lewis, *Mere Christianity* (London: Fontana, 1955), 148–49.

15. Henri Nouwen, *Turn My Mourning into Dancing: Moving through Hard Times with Hope* (Nashville, TN: Thomas Nelson, 2001), 90.

16. Ibid., 27, 43.

17. Ibid., 37, 63.

18. St. John of Damascus, *The Canon on the Transfiguration of the Lord*, qtd. in Andrew Louth, *St John Damascene: Tradition and Originality in Byzantine Theology*, Oxford Early Christian Studies (Oxford: Oxford University Press, 2002).

19. Ann Lewin, "Jeu d'Esprit," *Watching for the Kingfisher: Poems and Prayers* (Norwich: Canterbury, 2009), 91.

20. John Fischer, *Real Christians Don't Dance!* (London: Word, 1990), 123, 124, 119.

21. Sydney Carter, *Green Print for Song* (London: Stainer & Bell, 1974).

22. Donna Marie McGargill, "Servant Song."

5 The Energizing Language of Pilgrims and Travelers—(pages 46–56)

1. For an exploration of the journey image in relation to the cognitive theory of metaphor, see Olaf Jäkel, "Hypotheses Revisited: The Cognitive Theory of Metaphor Applied to Religious Texts," *Metaphorik* 2 (2002): 20–42. Jäkel identifies several key elements of the journey metaphor: the source of motion, the path

traversed, the goal in view, direction and making progress, landmarks, crossroads or forks in the path, and obstacles to be faced.

2. John Bunyan, *The Pilgrim's Progress in Today's English*, trans. J. H. Thomas (Eastbourne: Victory, 1972), 30.

3. Ibid.

4. Edwin Muir, "One Foot in Eden," *One Foot in Eden* (London: Faber and Faber, 1956), 46.

5. Arnold M. Eisen, *Galut: Modern Jewish Reflection on Homelessness and Homecoming* (Bloomington, IN: Indiana University Press, 1997).

6. Central Board of Finance of the Church of England, *Common Worship Initiation Services* (London: Church House, 1998).

7. *The Spiritual Exercises of St. Ignatius Loyola*, trans. Thomas Corbishley (Wheathampstead: Anthony Clarke, 1973), para. 23.

8. See William A. Barry and William J. Connolly, *The Practice of Spiritual Direction*, 2nd ed. (New York: Seabury, 2009), 85–106.

9. Kees Waaijman, *Spirituality: Forms, Foundations, Methods* (Leuven: Peeters, 2002), 131.

10. Kenneth Leech, *Soul Friend: Spiritual Direction in the Modern World* (London: Sheldon, 1977), 37.

11. Martin Thornton, *English Spirituality: An Outline of Ascetical Theology According to the English Pastoral Tradition* (Cambridge, MA: Cowley, 1986), 124.

12. Origen, *De Principiis*, qtd. in Andrew Louth, *The Origins of the Christian Mystical Tradition* (Oxford: Oxford University Press, 1981), 59. This section is indebted to Louth's exposition.

13. Ibid., 109.

14. Louis Bouyer, *A History of Christian Spirituality: Spirituality of the New Testament and the Fathers* (Tunbridge Wells: Burns & Oates, 1982), 393.

15. Stages of development in Christian spirituality are represented in the pioneering work of psychologists Erikson and Fowler. See Erik H. Erikson, *Childhood and Society* (London: Pelican, 1969), and *Identity and the Life Cycle* (New York: W. W. Norton, 1994); James W. Fowler, *Stages of Faith: The Psychology of Human Development and the Quest for Meaning*, rev. ed. (San Francisco: Harper, 1995). For a recent reworking of the Triple Way in the psychology of spirituality, see Benedict J. Groeschel, *Spiritual Passages: The Psychology of Spiritual Development* (New York: Crossroad, 1995). Another useful source is Elizabeth Liebert, *Changing Life Patterns: Adult Development in Spiritual Direction* (St. Louis: Chalice, 2000).

16. *John Climacus: The Ladder of Divine Ascent*, trans. Colm Luibheid and Norman Russell, Classics of Western Spirituality (Mahwah, NJ: Paulist Press, 1982), 259.

17. Robert Murray, *Symbols of Church and Kingdom: A Study in Early Syriac Tradition* (London: T & T Clark, 2006).

18. J. M. Harden, *The Anaphoras of the Ethiopic Liturgy* (London: SPCK, 1928), 66.

6 The Adventurous Language of Explorers and Seekers—(pages 57–64)

1. Qtd. in George A. Maloney, *Intoxicated with God: The Fifty Spiritual Homilies of Macarius* (Denville, NJ: Dimension, 1978), 33.

2. Joan Borysenko, in *A Woman's Journey to God* (New York: Riverhead, 2001), contrasts male spirituality represented in the ascent model of Jacob's ladder, with its successive linear stages, with female spirituality symbolised in Sarah's circle, a more relational, immanent model: less climbing, more nurturing!

3. For a critique of the ascent model see Margaret R. Miles, *The Image and Practice of Holiness: A Critique of the Classic Manuals of Devotion* (London: SCM, 1989).

4. *RB1980: The Rule of St. Benedict in English*, ed. Timothy Fry (Collegeville, MN: Liturgical Press, 1982), 32–38.

5. See *Gregory of Nyssa: The Life of Moses*, trans. Abraham J. Malherbe and Everett Ferguson, The Classics of Western Spirituality (New York: Paulist, 1978), 113–14.

6. See "On Perfection" in *From Glory to Glory: Texts from Gregory of Nyssa's Mystical Writings*, trans. Herbert Musurillo (New York: St. Vladimir's Seminary Press, 2001), 51–52. See also Andrew Louth, *The Origins of the Christian Mystical Tradition: From Plato to Denys* (Oxford: Oxford University Press, 2007).

7. Thérèse of Lisieux, *Story of a Soul*, qtd. in Jean C. J. d'Elbee, *I Believe in Love: A Personal Retreat based on the Teaching of St. Thérèse of Lisieux* (Manchester, NH: Sophia Institute, 2001), 27.

8. Catherine of Siena, *The Dialogue*, The Classics of Western Spirituality, trans. Suzanne Noffke (New York: Paulist, 1980). For a modern approach see Rosemary Gordon, *Bridges: Metaphor for Psychic Processes* (London: Karnac, 1993).

9. Alison M. Munro, "Aspects of Imagery in Catherine of Siena from a Jungian Perspective" (master's thesis, Rhodes University, 2001).

10. N. Gordon Cosby, *By Grace Transformed: Christianity for a New Millennium* (New York: Crossroad, 1998), 31.

11. Paul Tillich, *The Shaking of the Foundations* (New York: Charles Scribner, 1955), 55.

12. Richard J. Foster, *Celebration of Discipline: The Path to Spiritual Growth* (San Francisco: Harper, 1988), 1 .

13. *The Festal Menaion*, trans. Mother Mary and Kallistos Ware (London: Faber & Faber, 1969), 203.

14. Ibid., 205.

15. For other writers on depth spirituality see, for example, Yves Raguin, *The Depth of God*, trans. Kathleen England, The Religious Experiences Series 10 (Wheathampstead, Hertfordshire: Anthony Clarke, 1975); Mother Mary Clare, *Encountering the Depths: Prayer, Solitude, and Contemplation* (London: Darton, Longman & Todd, 1981); William P. Clemmons, *Discovering the Depths: Guidance in Spiritual Growth* (London: SPCK, 1989); Brother Ramon, *Deeper into God: A Handbook on Spiritual Retreats* (Basingstoke, Hampshire: Marshall Pickering, 1987).

7 The Creative Language of Builders and Citizens—(pages 65–73)

1. Thomas Traherne, "Felicity," quoted in *Happiness and Holiness: Thomas Traherne and his Writings*, ed. Denise Inge, Canterbury Studies in Spiritual Theology (Norwich: Canterbury, 2008), 112.

2. St. Teresa of Ávila, *Interior Castle*, trans. and ed. E. Allison Peers (London: Sheed & Ward, 1974), 1-2 .

3. Rowan Williams, *Teresa of Avila* (London: Continuum, 1991), 113-14.

4. St. Teresa of Ávila, *Interior Castle*, 6, 8. See also the more recent translation in *Teresa of Avila: The Interior Castle*, trans. Kieran Kavanaugh & Otilio Rodriguez (New York: Paulist, 1979).

5. Carolyn Humphreys, *From Ash to Fire: A Contemporary Journey through the Interior Castle of Teresa of Avila* (Hyde Park, NY: New City, 1992), 80. See also Tessa Bielecki, *Teresa of Avila: An Introduction to Her Life & Writings* (Tunbridge Wells, Kent: Burns & Oates, 1994).

6. St. Teresa of Ávila, *Interior Castle*, 33.

7. Verse 4 of Charles Wesley, "And can it be that I should gain," written shortly after his conversion experience in 1738.

8. Leonardo Boff, *Saint Francis: A Model of Human Liberation* (New York: Crossroad, 1990).

9. *Francis of Assisi: Early Documents*, vol. 1, *The Saint*, ed. Regis J. Armstrong, J. A. Wayne Hellman, and William J. Short (Hyde Park, NY: New City, 1999), 290.

10. Verses 1, 3, of Samuel Johnson, "City of God, How Broad and Far" (1860).

11. Bernard of Cluny, "Jerusalem the Golden," in *The Rhythm of Bernard de Morlaix, Monk of Cluny on the Celestial Country*, ed. and trans. J. Mason Neale (London: J. T. Hayes, 1865), 29.

12. Wayne A. Meeks, *The First Urban Christians: The Social World of the Apostle Paul* (New Haven: Yale University Press, 1983).

13. St. Augustine, *City of God*, ed. G. R. Evans, trans. Henry Bettenson, Penguin Classics (London: Penguin, 2003).

14. John Dominic Crossan, *God and Empire: Jesus against Rome, Then and Now* (San Francisco: HarperCollins, 2007).

8 The Sensuous Language of the Body—(pages 74–83)

1. Saint Augustine, *Confessions*, trans. Henry Chadwick (Oxford: Oxford University Press, 1991), 201.

2. Simeon the New Theologian, *On the Mystical Life: The Ethical Discourses*, vol. 2, trans. Alexander Golitzin (New York: St Vladimir's Seminary Press, 1996), 110.

3. *Catechism of the Catholic Church*, 2nd ed., no. 2562–63.

4. Joseph Ratzinger, "Theological Commentary" to Congregation for the Doctrine of the Faith, *The Message of Fatima* (June 26, 2006).

5. Hans Walter Wolff, *Anthropology of the Old Testament* (London: SCM, 1974).

6. John Cassian, *Conferences*, trans. Colm Luibheid, The Classics of Western Spirituality (New York: Paulist, 1985), 39, 41-42. See also John Cassian, *The Monastic Institutes: On the Training of a Monk and The Eight Deadly Sins*, trans. Jerome Bertram (London: Saint Austin, 1999).

7. Kallistos Ware, *The Inner Kingdom,* The Collected Works, vol. 1 (New York: St. Vladimir's Seminary Press, 2000), 62.

8. Kallistos Ware, "Ways of Prayer and Contemplation I: Eastern," in *Christian Spirituality: Origins to the Twelfth Century*, ed. Bernard McGinn, John Meyendorff, and Jean Leclercq, World Spirituality 16 (London: SCM, 1985), 401.

9. Archimandrite Ephraim of Vatopedi Monastery, "The Soul and Repentance," in *Friends of Mount Athos Annual Report 2006* (Oxford: Friends of Mount Athos, 2006).

10. Simeon the New Theologian, "Three Methods of Attention and Prayer," in *Writings from the Philokalia: On the Prayer of the Heart*, trans. E. Kadloubovsky & G. E. H. Palmer (London: Faber & Faber, 1977), 158.

11. Maximos the Confessor, "Four Hundred Texts on Love," in *The Philokalia: The Complete Text*, vol. 2, trans. G. E. H. Palmer, Philip Sherrard, and Kallistos Ware (London: Faber & Faber, 1981), 69.

12. Ibid., 74.

13. Qtd. in Sebastian P. Brock, *The Luminous Eye: The Spiritual World Vision of Saint Ephrem the Syrian* (Kalamazoo, MI: Cistercian, 1992), 73.

14. Qtd. in Brock, *Luminous Eye*, 75

15. Gregory of Nyssa, "Commentary on the Song of Songs," *From Glory to Glory: Texts from Gregory of Nyssa's Mystical Writings*, trans. Herbert Musurillo (London: John Murray, 1962), 156.

16. Bonaventure, *The Soul's Journey into God*, trans. Edwin Cousins, The Classics of Western Spirituality (New York: Paulist, 1978), 89.

17. *The Spiritual Exercises of Saint Ignatius: Saint Ignatius' Profound Precepts of Mystical Theology*, trans. Anthony Mottola (New York: Image, 1964).

18. George A. Maloney, *Intoxicated with God: The Fifty Spiritual Homilies of Macarius* (Denville, NJ: Dimension, 1980).

19. Hilarion Alfeyev, *The Spiritual World of Isaac the Syrian* (Kalamazoo, MI: Cistercian, 2000), 249.

20. Sue Woodruff, *Meditations with Mechthild of Magdeburg* (Sante Fe, NM: Bear, 1982), 88.

21. Jerome, *Letter to Heliodorus*, qtd. in Belden. C. Lane, *The Solace of Fierce Landscapes: Exploring Desert and Mountain Spirituality* (Oxford: Oxford University Press, 1998), 23.

22. Brock, *Luminous Eye*, 39.

23. A Franciscan Minor Pilgrim, *Order for the Procession in Jerusalem in the Basilica of the Holy Sepulchre of Our Lord Jesus Christ* (Jerusalem: Custodia Terrae Sanctae, undated).

24. The Celtic tradition develops this theme in different ways: the interweaving of threads in fabric can be a sign of the interpenetration of faith and life. Like threads, feelings can get tangled, and we may discern a pattern in the evolving design within the tapestry of our life.

25. Richard Rolheiser, *Seeking Spirituality: Guidelines for a Christian Spirituality for the Twenty-First Century* (London: Hodder & Stoughton, 1988), 137ff.

26. *The Collected Works of St. John of The Cross*, rev. ed., trans. Kieran Kavanaugh and Otilio Rodriguez (Washington: Institute of Carmelite Studies, 1991), 471.

27. John Follent, "Negative Experience and Christian Growth," in *St. John of the Cross: A Spirituality of Substance*, ed. Peter Slattery (New York: Alba House, 1994), 97.

28. *The Life of Saint Teresa of Avila by Herself*, trans. J. M. Cohen (London: Penguin, 1957), 210.

29. Columbanus, "Sermon Thirteen," in *Celtic Christian Spirituality: An Anthology of Medieval and Modern Sources*, ed. Oliver Davies and Fiona Bowie (London: SPCK, 1995).

30. Sebastian Brock, *The Syriac Fathers on Prayer and the Spiritual Life* (Kalamazoo, MI: Cistercian, 1987).

31. Robert Murray, *Symbols of Church and Kingdom: A Study in Early Syriac Tradition* (London: T & T Clark, 2006), 200.

32. John Bunyan, *The Pilgrim's Progress in Today's English*, trans. James H. Thomas (Eastbourne, East Sussex: Victory, 1972).

33. Dave Bilbrough, "I Am a New Creation" (© 1983 Thankyou Music).

34. Stephen Cherry, "Fullness of Life," *Barefoot Prayers: A Meditation a Day for Lent and Easter* (London: SPCK, 2013), 21.

9 The Archetypal Language of the Elements—(pages 84–96)

1. Qtd. in Esther de Waal, *The Celtic Way of Prayer: The Recovery of the Religious Imagination* (London: Hodder & Stoughton, 2003), 111.

2. Edwin Hatch, "Breath on Me, Breath of God," *Allon's Congregational Psalmist Hymnal*, ed. Henry Allon (London: Hodder & Stoughton, 1886), no. 220.

3. "Hymn on Faith 10," qtd. in Brock, *The Luminous Eye*, 108, 140.

4. Richard Rolle, *The Fire of Love*, trans. Clifton Wolters (London: Penguin, 1972). See also Rolle, *English Writings*, trans. Rosamund Allen, The Classics of Western Spirituality (New York: Paulist, 1988). Rolle has been called "the father of English literature"; his translations of the Bible were used by John Wycliffe in his preparation of the English Bible, and Rolle wrote many works both in Latin and his mother tongue. His poems, discourses, and scriptural commentaries reveal a debt to Augustine, Bernard, Bonaventure, and Richard of St. Victor. See Martin Thornton, *English Spirituality: An Outline of Ascetical Theology According to the English Pastoral Tradition* (Cambridge, MA: Cowley, 1986).

5. He writes about both physical sensations and psycho-auditory sensations, akin to locutions, as the hearing of a symphony of spiritual sounds or heavenly choirs that resonated somehow in his mind. He talks about experiencing sweetness of feeling in his body, and celebrates the emotions of wonder and joy, and of becoming "intoxicated with sweetness ever more rare" (*The Fire of Love*, 144). See Denis Reveney, *Language, Self and Love: Hermeneutics*

in the Writings of Richard Rolle and the Commentaries on the Song of Songs (Cardiff: University of Wales Press, 2001).

6. Letter 51, to Apostolic Nuncio of Tuscany, qtd. in *The Letters of St. Catherine of Sienna*, vol. 1, edited by Suzanne Noffke, Medieval & Renaissance Texts & Studies 52 (Binghamton, NY: Center for Medieval and Early Renaissance Studies, 1988), 153.

7. *The Collected Works of St John of the Cross*, 641–42.

8. Charles Wesley, "O Thou Who camest from above," *Short Hymns on Select Passages of the Holy Scriptures*, vol. 1 (Bristol: E. Farley, 1762).

9. Micheal O'Siadhail, "Talk," *Tongues* (Tarset, Northumberland: Bloodaxe, 2010), 132.

10. Paschal Canon in Holy Transfiguration Monastery, *The Pentecostarion* (Boston, MA: Holy Transfiguration Monastery, 1990), 29.

11. Benedicta Ward, *The Sayings of the Desert Fathers* (Kalamazoo, MI: Cistercian, 1975), 103.

12. A study of the Spanish mystics utilizes this image of the crucible: E. W. Trueman Dicken, *The Crucible of Love: A Study of the Mysticism of St. Teresa of Jesus and St. John of the Cross* (London: Sheed & Ward, 1963).

13. Sources stimulating our use of a river image include *The Gift of Rivers: True Stories of Life on the Water*, ed. Pamela Michael (San Francisco: Travelers' Tales, 2000); Theodore Graebner, *Sacred Waters: Modern Pilgrimages to the Fountains, Seas and Rivers of the Bible* (Whitefish, MT: Kessinger Reprints, 2003); William K. Tweedie, *Rivers and Lakes of Scripture* (London: T. Nelson, 1867).

14. James Roose-Evans, *The Inner Stage: Finding a Center in Prayer and Ritual* (Cambridge, MA: Cowley, 1990), 129.

15. Nerses Shnorhali, *Jesus, the Son*, trans. Mischa Kudian (London: Mashtots, 1986), 45 .

16. Qtd. in John Meyendorff, *St. Gregory Palamas and Orthodox Spirituality* (New York: St Vladimir's Seminary Press, 1974), 49 .

17. *Interior Castle* 4.2.2. See also E. Allison Peers, *Mother of Carmel: A Portrait of St. Teresa of Jesus* (London: SCM, 1945), 54. See also Teresa's *Life*, chap. 11.

18. Teresa of Avila, *Interior Castle* (London: Sheed and Ward, 1974), 37.

19. John Newton, "Glorious Things of Thee Are Spoken," *Olney Hymns in Three Books*, vol. 1, *On Select Texts of Scripture* (London: W. Oliver, 1779), no. 60.

20. See Ian Matthew, *The Impact of God: Soundings from St John of the Cross* (London: Hodder & Stoughton, 1995), 72.

21. John of the Cross, *The Collected Works*, 177.

22. Priscilla J. Owens, "Will Your Anchor Hold" (1882).

23. John Mason, "How Shall I Sing That Majesty," *Spiritual Songs, or Songs of Praise to Almighty God upon Several Occasions* (London: 1683).

24. F. W. Faber, "Come to Jesus," *Hymns*, 2nd ed. (London: Thomas Richardson, 1862), no. 102.

25. Qtd. in Matthew Fox, *Meditations with Meister Eckhart* (Rochester, VT: Bear, 1983), 49. For a useful anthology, see Meister Eckhart, *The Man from Whom God Hid Nothing*, ed. Ursula Fleming (London: Collins, 1988).

26. Fox, *Meditations with Meister Eckhart*, 110.

27. From the Black Book of Carmarthen, qtd. in *Celtic Fire: An Anthology of Celtic Christian Literature*, ed. Robert Van de Weyer (London: Darton, Longman & Todd, 1990), 92.

28. John Donne, "Holy Sonnets V," in *The Poems of John Donne*, edited by Herbert Grierson (Oxford: Oxford University Press, 1933), 295.

10 The Challenging Language of Struggle—(pages 97–106)

1. This language has been described as "warlike, military, destructive, dividing" in Arthur L. Clements, *Poetry of Contemplation: John Donne, George Herbert, Henry Vaughan, and the Modern Period* (Albany, NY: State University of New York Press, 1990), 72.

2. This chapter is indebted to Andrew D. Mayes, *Spirituality of Struggle: Pathways to Growth* (London, SPCK, 2002).

3. Charles Wesley, "Soldiers of Christ, Arise," *Hymns and Sacred Poems*, vol. 1 (Bristol: Felix Farley, 1749).

4. Gerhard von Rad, *Genesis*, 3rd ed. (London: SCM, 1972), 325.

5. It evokes both the creation account of order emerging from the waters of chaos (Gen 1) and the Exodus story of liberation where foes were drowned in the waters of the Red Sea and where a barrier became a crossing-place. It also recalls the Old Testament theme of dragons and demons lurking in the dark waters (Job 41:1; Ps 74:14). There is a debate, however, about the extent of the symbolism in the text. Fokkelman, for example, sees symbolism in the crossing, the darkness, and the rising sun. Jan P. Fokkelman, *Narrative Art in Genesis: Specimens of Stylistic and Structural Analysis*, 2nd ed. (Sheffield: JSOT Press, 1991), 208ff.

6. Henri J. M. Nouwen, *The Way of the Heart: The Spirituality of the Desert Fathers* (London: Darton, Longman & Todd, 1981), 31.

7. Henri J. M. Nouwen, *Ministry and Spirituality: Creative Ministry, the Wounded Healer, Reaching Out* (New York: Continuum, 1998), 161.

8. Walter Brueggemann, *Genesis*, Interpretation (Atlanta: John Knox, 1982), 270–71.

9. George Herbert, "Sion," *The Complete English Works* (London: David Campbell, 1995), 103.

10. Herbert, "Prayer I," *The Complete English Works*, 49.

11. Herbert, in a letter to Nicholas Ferrar, qtd. in *The Complete English Works*, xv.

12. Herbert, "Evensong," *The Complete English Works*, 61.

13. Herbert, "The Collar," *The Complete English Works*, 149.

14. Herbert, "Longing," *The Complete English Works*, 145.

15. Herbert, "Love III," *The Complete English Works*, 184.

16. Herbert, "Redemption," *The Complete English Works*, 37.

17. Herbert, "The Cross," *The Complete English Works*, 160.

18. For contemporary writers on this theme see Henri M. Nouwen, *Ministry and Spirituality* (New York: Continuum, 1998) and Esther de Waal, *Living with Contradiction: An Introduction to Benedictine Spirituality* (Norwich: Canterbury, 1989).

11 Contemporary Language of Change and Transformation— (pages 107–15)

1. Simon Brading and Jules Burt, "Creator God (No One Better)" (© 2011 Thankyou Music); live recording on Newday, *We Are Yours: Live Worship from NewDay 2011* (© 2011 Integrity Music).

2. *The Worship Songbook 2* (Eastbourne: Kingsway, 2012). See also *More Dreams Alive: Prayers by Teenagers*, ed. Carl Koch (Winona, MN: Saint Mary's Press, 1995). For helpful information on the affective life of certain generations, see Sara Savage, Sylvia Collins-Mayo, and Bob Mayo, *Making Sense of Generation Y: The World View of 15–25-Year-Olds*, Explorations (London: Church House, 2006); Sylvia Collins-Mayo, Bob Mayo, and Sally Nash, *The Faith of Generation Y*, Explorations (London: Church House, 2010); Wendy Murray Zoba, *Generation 2k: What Parents & Others Need to Know about the Millennials* (Downers Grove, IL: InterVarsity, 1999).

3. Paul Baloche, Ed Kerr, Alyssa Mellinger, and Sheila Rabe, "My Hope" (© 2012 Integrity Music).

4. Brading and Burt, "Creator God (No One Better)" (© 2011 Thankyou Music).

5. Ben Cantelon, Nick Herbert, and Tim Hughes, "Everything in Color" (© 2011 Thankyou Music).

6. Anthony Hoisington, Chris Hoisington, Leslie Jordan, and David Leonard, "Alive" (© 2011 Integrity Music).

7. Rend Collective Experiment, "Christ Has Set Me Free" (© 2011 Thankyou Music).

8. Travis Ryan, Brandon Collins, and Matt Redman, "Chase" (© 2012 Integrity Music).

9. Kathryn Scott, "We Still Believe" (© 2010 Integrity Music).

10. Sam Blake, Stephen Gibson, Joel Pridmore, and Ian Yates, "We Will Be a Church (Authentic Church)" (© 2012 Thankyou Music).

11. Trevor Whittock, *Metaphor and Film*, Cambridge Studies in Film (Cambridge: Cambridge University Press, 2009).

12. Robert Moore and Douglas Gillette, *The King Within: Accessing the King in the Male Psyche* (New York: Harper & Row, 1989), 33.

13. Sherry Turkle, *Life on the Screen: Identity in the Age of the Internet* (London: Simon & Schuster, 1997).

14. John Twisleton, *Using the Jesus Prayer: Steps to a Simpler Christian Life* (London: Bible Reading Fellowship, 2014), 95.

15. Frederick R. C. Clarke and Richard Granville Jones, "God of Concrete" (© 1968 Stainer & Bell).

16. Rend Collective Experiment, "Praise Like Fireworks" (© 2011 Thankyou Music).

17. Cynthia Bourgeault, *The Wisdom Jesus: Transforming Heart and Mind—A New Perspective on Christ and His Message* (London: Shambhala, 2008), 33–36.

12 Language of Darkness and Cloud: Beyond Words and Images— (pages 116–22)

1. John Greenleaf Whittier, "First-Day Thoughts," *The Complete Works of John Greenleaf Whittier: Poems*, vol. 2 (Boston: Houghton, Mifflin, 1892), 242.

2. Meister Eckhart, *The Man from Whom God Hid Nothing*, 90.

3. Jean Danielou, Introduction to *From Glory to Glory: Texts from Gregory of Nyssa's Mystical Writings*, trans. Herbert Musurillo (London: John Murray, 1962), 27.

4. Gregory of Nyssa, *The Life of Moses*, trans. Abraham J. Malherbe and Everett Ferguson, The Classics of Western Spirituality (New York: Paulist, 1978), 95.

5. Jean Danielou, "Introduction," 30. Gregory also develops this in reference to his interpretation of the Song of Songs where the divine darkness is characterized not only by unknowing but also by desire and yearning on the part of the bride.

6. Andrew Louth, *The Origins of the Christian Mystical Tradition: From Plato to Denys* (Oxford: Oxford University Press, 1981), 91.

7. Pseudo-Dionysius, "The Mystical Theology," in *The Complete Works*, trans. Colm Luibheid, Classics of Western Spirituality (New York: Paulist, 1987), 135 . See also Andrew Louth, *Denys the Aeropagite*, Outstanding Christian Thinkers (New York: Continuum, 1989).

8. Pseudo-Dionysius, "The Mystical Theology," 135.

9. See Bernard McGinn, *The Foundation of Mysticism: Origins to the Fifth Century*, The Presence of God: A History of Western Christian Mysticism 1 (London: SCM, 1991).

10. *The Collected Works of St John of the Cross*, 120.

11. Rowan Williams, *The Wound of Knowledge: Christian Spirituality from the New Testament to Saint John of the Cross* (Cambridge, MA: Cowley, 1991), 172-173, 180.

12. *The Cloud of Unknowing and Other Works*, trans. Clifton Wolters (London: Penguin, 1976), 60. For a more recent translation see *The Cloud of Unknowing*, trans. James Walsh, The Classics of Western Spirituality (New York: Paulist, 1981). See also David Lonsdale, "The Cloud of Unknowing," in *Traditions of Spiritual Guidance*, ed. Lavinia Byrne (Collegeville, MN: Liturgical Press, 1990).

13. *The Cloud of Unknowing*, trans. Wolters, 51. For a consideration of the role of desire in spirituality see Philip Sheldrake, *Befriending Our Desires* (London: Darton, Longman & Todd, 1994).

14. *The Cloud of Unknowing*, trans. Wolters, 110.

15. Ibid., 61.

16. Ibid., 106–7.

17. Ibid., 53–54.

18. Bernard of Clairvaux, "*Jesu dulcis memoria*," in *Lyra Catholica*, trans. Edward Caswall (London: Levey, Robson, and Franklyn, 1849), 56–57.